iPhone 15
SENIORS GUIDE

A Complete, Easy-to-Follow Manual to Master Your New Device. Discover All Features with Illustrated Step-by-Step Instructions & Helpful Tips to Maximize Your iPhone Experience

- ✓ **New Features of iOS 17**
- ✓ **Camera Settings**
- ✓ **Configure SOS**
- **Tips & Tricks**
- ✓ **Apple Maps**
- ✓ **Apple Pay**
- **SIRI**

Vin Mayer

Table of Contents

INTRODUCTION

This is the comprehensive guide to Apple's newest masterpiece in the world of smartphones, the iPhone 15, and we would like to use this time to welcome you to it. This comprehensive book is meant to increase your understanding and mastery of the iPhone 15, regardless of whether you are a first-time iPhone user or an Apple devotee with years of experience. This is because the guide covers a wide range of topics, each of which is broken down into more specific sections. The iPhone 15 is more than just a phone; it is a tremendous instrument that has the capability of radically altering the way in which you live your life, conduct your business, and interact with the rest of the world. The Apple iPhone 15 is more than simply a phone because of its groundbreaking features, fashionable design, and cutting-edge technologies.

In order to gain a deeper comprehension of the iPhone 15, we are going to spend the majority of this tutorial exploring the numerous features, functions, and capabilities that the iPhone 15 possesses. Every aspect of the iPhone 15, from its jaw-dropping display to its powerful A15 Bionic CPU, from its cutting-edge camera system to its perfect integration with iOS 15, will be studied in excruciating detail. This includes every aspect of the device. Whether you want to take images that are just spectacular, boost the amount of work you get done, or research the newest applications and features, this book is your passport to unlocking the full potential of your iPhone 15.

Our goal is to make sure that you have access to the necessary knowledge and training so that you can make the most of your time spent using the iPhone 15. You will be able to manage the iPhone 15 with ease and self-assurance if you follow the step-by-step instructions, expert suggestions, and tactics for troubleshooting that are presented throughout this book. We will go over everything, from establishing a connection to your device to becoming adept with its most complicated capabilities, in order to ensure that you are prepared to take on any task or barrier that may come your way.

Therefore, whether you are a novice when it comes to technology or an experienced iPhone user, you should fasten your seatbelts and get ready to explore the magnificent universe that the iPhone 15 has to offer. It will blow your mind. Let's not waste any time and go straight to the bottom of what this great technology has in store for us by investigating the myriad of alternatives that are at our disposal right now. Your adventure with the iPhone 15 begins right this very second.

CHAPTER ONE
WHAT ARE THE DIFFERENCES AMONG IPHONE 15

- Design: With each new iPhone release, Apple typically improves the design by making the devices thinner, lighter, or introducing new materials or finishes. Apple also often refines the design.

- Display: Updates may contain enhancements in display technology, such as greater color accuracy, improved brightness, or higher resolutions. These kinds of enhancements could be provided in an update.
- Apple is continuously attempting to improve the capabilities of its cameras by introducing new features, producing better outcomes in low light, and increasing the amount of megapixels available.
- Processor: Typically, Apple provides newer generations of the iPhone with a more powerful and energy-efficient processor. This results in enhanced overall performance as well as a longer battery life.
- Software: Whenever a new iPhone is released, It often comes with the most recent version of iOS, which comes with its own collection of newly developed features and updates.
- Battery Life: Apple may optimize both the hardware and software of future iPhone models in order to give longer battery lives for users.
- Special Features Each model of the iPhone may come with its own collection of one-of-a-kind features. For example, the Pro models often contain additional technologies such as

LiDAR scanners, which improve the quality of augmented reality experiences; ProMotion displays, which make graphics appear more fluid; and various camera lenses, which enable advanced shooting possibilities.

- Options for Storage: Apple will occasionally update the available storage options for each iPhone model, delivering either more or less capacity at varied price points. This is done in order to fulfill customer demand.

FEATURES OF IPHONE 15

NEW MATERIALS, SIZES, AND ERGONOMICS

The iPhone 15 flaunts a revolutionary design by incorporating premium materials including as reinforced glass, aerospace-grade aluminum, or ceramic into its construction. The device accommodates a wide range of user choices because it comes in two different sizes: 6.1 inches and 6.7 inches. Because of the wide range of sizes available, users are able to select a device that is an ideal fit for their hands, which contributes to an improved ergonomic experience overall. The thoughtful application of these materials, in conjunction with careful consideration of the device's dimensions and ergonomics, has resulted in a product that is not only beautiful to look at but also a delight to operate.

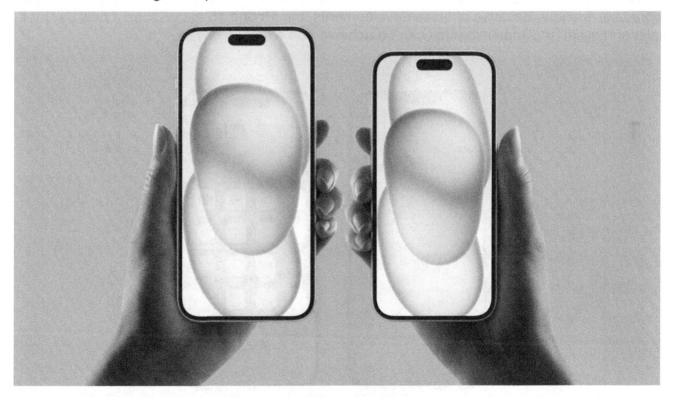

SIGNIFICANT ALTERATIONS MADE TO THE DESIGN

The design of the iPhone 15 has been updated with a number of significant improvements that differentiate it from its predecessors. One important modification is the narrowing of the space between the screen and the bezels, which results in a more immersive display that fills the entire screen.

The lack of a physical home button improves the screen-to-body ratio, giving users access to a display area that is both larger and more compelling than before. In addition, the notch on the front of the device has been relocated or shrunk, increasing the amount of usable screen real estate while maintaining all of the necessary front-facing sensors and cameras. Both the positioning and the design of the back camera module have been precisely created to ensure that aesthetics and functionality are in perfect alignment with one another. Not only do these design enhancements boost the iPhone 15's visual appeal, but they also contribute to an enhanced user experience, making it a standout choice among the options available in the smartphone market. Size variants also play a role in elevating the iPhone 15's visual appeal.

AN OVERVIEW OF ADVANCED DISPLAY TECHNOLOGY

The display technology featured on the iPhone 15 is state-of-the-art, and it reimagines what it means to have a visual experience. Because it makes use of cutting-edge OLED technology, the gadget is capable of producing blacker blacks and colors that are more brilliant, so giving users an unrivaled viewing experience.

This cutting-edge display technology ensures higher contrast ratios and faster response times, making it an excellent choice for gaming, as well as for the consumption of multimedia and the performance of other tasks. The incorporation of ProMotion technology provides silky smooth scrolling and fluid interactions, further enhancing the display's responsiveness and making it more user-friendly. Because of these developments, the iPhone 15 establishes a new bar for the level of realism and immersion that can be achieved on a mobile device.

ENHANCEMENTS TO THE BRIGHTNESS AND COLOR ACCURACY

The display of the iPhone 15 features considerable improvements in both color accuracy and brightness, making it one of the most notable characteristics of the device. The gadget reproduces both still photos and moving videos with an extraordinary level of fidelity, delivering colors that are true to life.

Users can anticipate images that are rich, colorful, and faithful to the intentions of the designer regardless of whether they are editing photos, watching movies, or browsing the internet. Additionally, the iPhone 15 improves outdoor visibility by increasing the brightness levels, which ensures that the display can be easily read even when the sun is shining brightly. Because of these advancements, not only is the overall viewing experience improved, but users also receive a display that is optimized for a variety of lighting settings. As a result, the iPhone 15 is an excellent option for those who prioritize having a device with high-quality display.

A NEW A16 BIONIC CHIP FROM THE A-SERIES

The state-of-the-art A16 Bionic chip is the driving force behind the remarkable performance of the iPhone 15. This chip, which was meticulously designed and developed, exemplifies Apple's most recent and groundbreaking technological achievements. The A16 Bionic includes sophisticated processing cores, high-performance graphics processing units (GPUs), and dedicated artificial intelligence engines.

It is built on an architecture that is highly efficient. Because of the complementary nature of its components, the iPhone 15 is able to easily complete difficult activities thanks to the lightning-fast speeds and unrivaled efficiency that they provide. In addition to delivering extraordinary raw power, the A16 Bionic chip also optimizes energy management. As a result, the device's battery life is extended as it continues to deliver excellent performance.

IMPROVED SPEED, MULTITASKING, AND GAMING

The A16 Bionic chip that is built into the iPhone 15 ushers in a new era of speed, allowing for fluid multitasking and gaming experiences that are more immersive. As a result of the device's improved CPU and GPU capabilities, it is able to handle resource-intensive programs with ease. This enables users to seamlessly switch between applications, edit high-resolution films, and play graphics-intensive games without experiencing any hiccups.

The sophisticated neural engine of the chip enables AI-driven features, which improves a wide variety of aspects, including computational photography and facial recognition. This level of performance not only increases productivity but also offers players unrivaled responsiveness, graphics that are realistic, and gaming that is seamless. The expanded speed and multitasking capabilities of the iPhone 15 offer a seamless and efficient user experience, regardless of whether users are editing material, juggling multiple apps, or indulging in mobile gaming.

SPECIFICATIONS AND CAPABILITIES OF THE CAMERA

The iPhone 15 has amazing camera specifications and a number of cutting-edge capabilities, both of which push the boundaries of what is possible with mobile photography. Because it has sensors with a high resolution, the gadget is capable of capturing fine details and vibrant colors, which results in excellent photographs and videos. The combination of improved optical image stabilization (OIS) and larger pixel sizes enables remarkable low-light performance.

This enables users to produce photographs that are clear and sharp regardless of the lighting conditions they are shooting in. In addition, the camera system of the iPhone 15 includes a flexible range of focal lengths, which enables users to record wide-angle vistas, detailed close-ups, and telephoto pictures with the level of precision found in professional equipment. The device produces extraordinary depth of field and dynamic range as a consequence of breakthroughs in aperture management and sensor technology. As a result, the images produced by the device are nothing short of spectacular.

SOPHISTICATED PHOTOGRAPHY AND VIDEOGRAPHY MODES

The iPhone 15 goes beyond the capabilities of traditional photography by providing a wealth of sophisticated photography and videography modes that are geared toward photography enthusiasts as well as professional videographers. Innovative features such as the Night mode have been improved, making it possible for users to take photographs with astonishing levels of clarity even in low-light settings. Additionally, the gadget introduces ProRAW capabilities, which allow users to capture photographs in a high-quality RAW format and retain more data for greater post-processing flexibility. These capabilities may be found on the device. The iPhone 15 brings a number of ground-breaking innovations in the world of filmmaking, one of which is called Cinematic Mode.

This mode provides depth effects and focuses shifts in a smooth manner, just like a professional movie camera would. Even while shooting in unpredictable environments, smooth and stable footage may be achieved with the help of high-quality 8K video recording and sophisticated image stabilization technology. Users of the iPhone 15 are given the ability to unleash their creativity and capture memories in ways that were previously thought to be impossible on a mobile device thanks to the enhanced photography and videography modes included in the device.

BATTERY LIFE AND OPTIMIZATION

The iPhone 15 comes with a considerable increase in battery life, which is made possible by sophisticated optimizations in both the hardware and the software. The appliance makes use of the most recent innovations in technology to achieve the highest possible efficiency in terms of power consumption. Users will be able to use their devices for longer periods of time without having to recharge them as frequently if the battery capacity is increased and sophisticated power management is implemented.

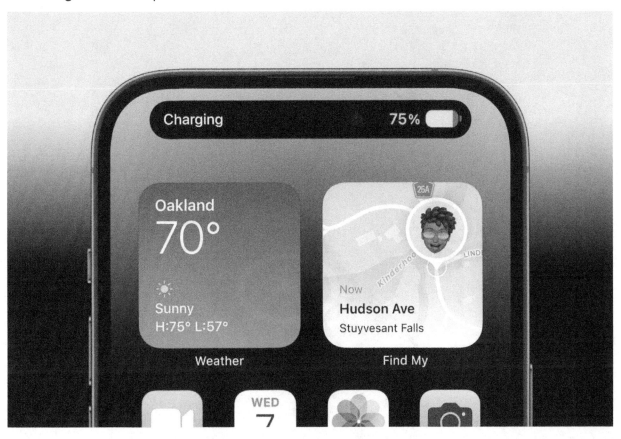

The improved battery life of the iPhone 15 makes it possible for customers to rely on their device throughout the day, even if they put a significant amount of strain on it by performing activities such as heavy web surfing, video streaming, or productivity work.

CHARGING CAPABILITIES THAT ARE BOTH QUICK AND WIRELESS

The iPhone 15 not only has a longer battery life, but it also has the ability to charge more quickly, so you can quickly top off your battery. Users are able to get a significant battery boost in just a few minutes if the device supports fast charging, which ensures that the gadget is ready to use whenever it is required to do so. In addition, consumers may charge their iPhone 15 without having to fumble with cables because the smartphone is compatible with wireless charging, which is a helpful feature.

Users who have a device that is compatible with Qi wireless charging pads can simply place their device on a charging mat to enjoy a cable-free and seamless charging experience on their device. These characteristics of quick charging and wireless charging not only improve user convenience, but they also enable flexibility, enabling users to charge their smartphone in the manner that is most appropriate for their way of life.

IMPROVEMENT TO 5G, WI-FI 6E AND BLUETOOTH

The iPhone 15 is at the vanguard of connection, enabling consumers blisteringly fast internet rates and a frictionless transmission of data. Users will be able to experience extremely fast download and upload rates, as well as low latency and dependable connections, thanks to the increased capabilities of 5G. This will make it possible for users to stream content without interruption and play online games more quickly. Additionally, the gadget is compatible with Wi-Fi 6E, which is the most recent version of the Wi-Fi standard.

This version offers higher bandwidth, decreased interference, and quicker data transmission speeds, particularly in crowded places. In addition, Bluetooth connectivity has been enhanced, making it possible to establish connections with a wider variety of devices—from headphones to smart home technology—in a quicker and more dependable manner. The improvements made to 5G, Wi-Fi, and Bluetooth technologies will ensure that users of the iPhone 15 will have a connection experience that is streamlined and quick to respond.

SUPPORT FOR DUAL SIM CARDS AND eSIM

When it comes to cellular connectivity, the Apple iPhone 15 offers both versatility and ease. It supports dual SIM cards, which enables customers to make use of a single device to manage two different phone numbers. This is especially helpful for people who want to keep their professional and personal relationships separate, as well as for frequent fliers who make use of local SIM cards while traveling internationally.

Additionally, the gadget supports eSIM technology, which enables users to activate a cellular plan without the need for a physical SIM card. This is made possible by the fact that users do not need to physically insert a SIM card. This functionality of digital SIM cards makes the process of activation much easier and gives users more alternatives for selecting and maintaining their cellular subscriptions. The iPhone 15 is designed to accommodate a wide range of user requirements by supporting not only dual SIM cards but also electronic SIM cards. This allows customers to maintain their connections in the manner that is most convenient for them.

IPHONE 15 TIPS AND TRICKS

Use the Action button to recognize music (15 Pro/ 15 Pro Max only)

The previous mute switch on the iPhone 15 Pro has been replaced with the new Action Button, which gives you access to a variety of features and functions, including the ability to activate the torch, record a voice note, and start the camera. However, you can also utilize it for Siri Shortcuts, which enables it to perform a plethora of useful operations that were not previously available.

One that I found to be particularly helpful was the integration of Shazam; all I had to do was press and hold the button to identify music that was being played nearby. If you have Shazam installed, navigate to Settings > Action Button, scroll through to shortcut, and then select the shortcut choice from the menu that appears. Find the option that says "recognize music," and you'll see a button labeled "Shazam." When you press and hold it, it will show the Shazam music identification graphic in your Dynamic Island and then tell you when it has located the tune you are looking for. Check out our in-depth guide if you want to learn more about the Action Button.

Drag multiple apps into a folder at once

By tapping and holding one app icon, dragging it, and then tapping on other icon while holding it, you may quickly and conveniently drag a selection of apps into one folder. This can be done by tapping and holding one app icon. After selecting all of the additional applications that you wish to relocate, just drag the collection into an existing folder and then let go of the mouse button.

Only charge to 80%

Charging a battery just until it reaches 80 percent capacity is recommended if you want it to last for a long period and remain in good health. This is now possible thanks to a new setting in iOS that you may adjust. To turn it on, go to Settings > Battery > Battery Health and Charging, and then choose Charging Optimisation from the menu that appears after that. Choose the limit of 80% from the list of available possibilities.

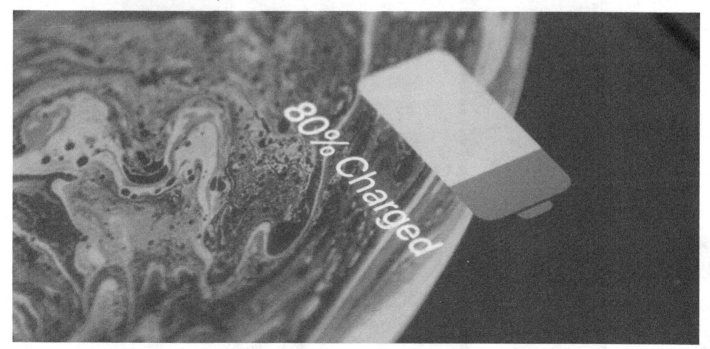

Generate rain sounds with a button press

Simply pressing a button will produce sounds of rain.

By pressing the side button three times in quick succession, users of iOS devices have the power to create background sounds for their apps. To begin, you will need to select the sound that you want it to produce. To do this, navigate to Settings > Accessibility > Audio/Vision and then click on Background Sounds. Now, select the sound effect you want it to play by tapping the 'Sound' button and selecting it from the list of available possibilities.

Go return to the Accessibility settings list and tap the 'Accessibility Shortcut' button in order to activate the ability to play that sound by pressing the side button on your iPhone. If you triple-click the side key when 'Background Sounds' is selected from the drop-down menu, the game will play the sound you specified.

Text can be captured and translated using the camera

There is a feature in the camera that can automatically detect when you are pointing it at text. As soon as your phone realizes there is text in the camera view, you'll see a little icon appear that looks like three lines in an outlined square. Tapping it that icon will grab the text, then give you the option to copy it, select it all, look it up, translate it, or share it. You can even drag to highlight a specific portion and peep

The most straightforward approach to picture editing.

There is a fairly simple way to crop into your images on your iPhone, so you won't have to waste time going through the many photo editing tools and cropping in that manner. Simply navigate to Photos, locate and open the desired image, and use your fingers to pinch and zoom in until the image's borders touch the screen's edge. Once you get it the size you want, hit the 'Crop' button in the top right corner of the screen. Alternatively, you can tap and hold it to choose a predetermined aspect ratio, and then tap the 'Crop' button to set it to the ratio you selected. When you are satisfied, press the done button.

Do a search for "laundry care icons"

With the release of iOS 17, Visual Look Up gained a significant amount of intelligence, expanding its recognition capabilities beyond historical landmarks, flora, and animals. If you take a picture of a laundry care label, for example, then tap the Visual Look Up 'i' icon with stars in the bottom toolbar under the image, and then click Visual Look Up from the pop-up menu, it will show you what the laundry care icons mean on that particular label. If you take a picture of a food label, it will show you what the food icon means.

Make a button out of the Apple logo to hide it.

You can capture a screenshot or activate another function on your iPhone by pressing the back of the phone near the Apple logo, provided that the appropriate settings are turned on. Navigate to the "Settings" menu, then "Accessibility," then "Touch," and finally, "Back Tap." Now, choose one of the functions from the list of options for the double tap. I went with Screenshot, but you are free to select anything else that strikes your fancy. A triple tap can also be accomplished by adding one.

CHAPTER TWO
FEATURES OF IOS 17

In the ever-evolving landscape of technology, Apple has consistently pushed the boundaries of innovation, transforming how we interact with our devices and the digital world. With the introduction of iOS 17, Apple continues its legacy of excellence, bringing forth a mobile operating system that not only enhances the functionality of its devices but also redefines the way users engage with their iPhones and iPads.

AN OVERVIEW OF APPLE'S LATEST OPERATING SYSTEM, IOS 17, AS IT APPLIES TO APPLE DEVICES

iOS 17 is in the vanguard of Apple's software advancements, and it exemplifies the company's dedication to improve the digital experience for millions of customers all over the world. iOS 17, the most recent version of Apple's industry-leading operating system, presents consumers with a plethora of innovative new features that are intended to reimagine the ways in which they interact with their iPhones, iPads, and other Apple-made products.

This operating system is a major step forward, using cutting-edge technology to provide users with an experience that is streamlined, user-friendly, and individualized to their specific needs.

THE SIGNIFICANCE OF IOS 17 IN ENHANCING BOTH THE USER EXPERIENCE AND THE FUNCTIONAL CAPABILITIES OF THE DEVICE

The new iOS 17 is not merely an update; rather, it is a complete overhaul. It plays a crucial part in improving the entire user experience as well as the operation of the device, catering to the requirements of users in a digital landscape that is always shifting. iOS 17, with its emphasis on customization, privacy, communication, and efficiency, gives consumers the ability to modify their devices to better suit their lifestyles.

This makes for an experience that is more fluid, intuitive, and pleasurable for all parties involved. Apple's commitment to providing its customers with an ecosystem that is safe, effective, and enjoyable is reaffirmed by the company's focus on designing products with the user in mind and including innovative features.

STATEMENT REGARDING THE TRANSITION

We are going to do a thorough investigation into iOS 17, looking into its most important new features and improvements, as outlined in this outline. The way in which customers use their Apple devices will be completely rethought thanks to the several functionalities that are included in iOS 17, which range from a reimagined home screen to enhanced privacy settings. Join us as we explore these innovations in order to reveal the ways in which iOS 17 reshapes the digital landscape and transforms the mundane into the remarkable. Let's take a look into the future of iOS, which is where innovation and user experience will intersect in a way that will take the way we engage with our iPhones, iPads, and other Apple products to a whole new level.

INTRODUCTION OF THE REDESIGNED HOME SCREEN LAYOUT

iOS 17 introduces a redesigned home screen layout, which offers a user interface that is easier to use and more organized. The newly revamped home screen improves usability by allowing for faster access to programs that are regularly used as well as information that is essential. The layout is well thought out, which ensures that the most important components are presented in a prominent manner, which in turn simplifies navigation and improves user productivity.

HIGHLY CUSTOMIZABLE WIDGETS AND THE FUNCTIONALITIES

They Provide One of the improvements that really stands out in iOS 17 is the level of customization available for the widgets. Users have the ability to personalize their home screens by adding widgets of varying sizes. These widgets give users the ability to display information in real time from their preferred applications.

These widgets provide users with a variety of dynamic material, including current weather conditions, upcoming events, news headlines, and fitness statistics. Widgets can be resized and rearranged by users in accordance with their individual tastes, allowing users to personalize their home screens to meet their specific requirements and interests. This level of customisation not only improves the appearance of the device, but it also gives users immediate access to important data without requiring them to open any specific applications first.

SMART STACKS AND WIDGET SUGGESTIONS FOR A MORE PERSONALIZED USER EXPERIENCE

The addition of Smart Stacks and Widget Suggestions in iOS 17 takes the concept of personalisation to a whole new level. The Smart Stacks feature allows users to dynamically curate widgets based on their usage patterns, providing information that is pertinent at various times of the day. For instance, it may display a widget for your calendar in the morning, news headlines during the middle of the day, and your fitness progress in the evening. Users will automatically receive content that is pertinent to their context because to this adaptability, which eliminates the need for human modifications.

The Widget Suggestions feature examines the actions taken by users and recommends widgets that are relevant to their activities. For users who are in the habit of checking the day's forecast first thing in the morning, iOS 17 may recommend adding a weather widget to their home screen. Because of these user-friendly characteristics, the home screen is not just a static display but rather a personalized center of information and functionality for the user. This ensures that the user will have a more positive experience when using the device. The revamped home screen and widgets in iOS 17 have redefined the user interaction experience, making it more user-friendly, user-focused, and efficient.

AN OVERVIEW OF THE SPATIAL AUDIO AND VOICE ISOLATION FEATURES AVAILABLE IN FACETIME CALLS

iOS 17 introduces spatial audio and speech separation, which ushers in a new era for FaceTime calls. The use of spatial audio recreates the experience of listening to natural sounds by giving the impression that speech is emanating from the direction in which each individual is located on the screen. This results in an atmosphere of communication that is more immersive and true to life. In addition, technology that isolates the speaker's voice decreases distracting background noise, allowing the listener to concentrate entirely on the speaker's words. Because of these enhancements, FaceTime calls are now not just aesthetically appealing but also sonically immersive. This contributes to an increased sense of presence and connection throughout talks.

THE FEATURES OF THE NEW ACTION BUTTON

The higher-tier iPhone 15 Pro and iPhone 15 Pro Max models have introduced a novel feature, replacing the traditional ring/silent switch that has been a fixture on iPhones since their inception. This new feature is called the "action button," and it offers customization options, allowing you to execute various functions swiftly. These functions include activating the flashlight, launching the camera, and recording voice memos.

However, it's important to note that the action button can only perform one function at a time. If you wish to switch it to another function, you'll need to access your settings and reassign the button each time.

Some iPhone 15 Pro users have proposed an enhancement to make the action button more versatile. They suggest enabling the action button to switch between functions based on the phone's state, making it more intuitive. For example, the action button could toggle between functions depending on whether "Do Not Disturb" mode is enabled or disabled, or it could respond differently when "Low Power" mode is turned on or off.

While the standard iPhone 15 doesn't currently offer this capability out of the box, there's a workaround to "hack" the action button to perform multiple functions based on your phone's orientation. Below, you'll find a guide on how to achieve this:

1. Begin by downloading the "Orientation Action Mode" shortcut, which alters the action button's behavior based on your phone's orientation. This shortcut allows the action

button to trigger different actions depending on whether your iPhone is held horizontally, vertically, or face down.

2. To add this shortcut to your library, follow these steps:

   - Download the "Orientation Action Mode" shortcut for your iPhone 15 Pro or Pro Max.

   - Select "Get Shortcut" and then "Add Shortcut" to incorporate it into your Shortcut library.

3. Additionally, you'll need to download the "Actions" app from the App Store. This app, developed by Sindre Sorhus, provides supplementary actions for your shortcuts, enhancing the functionality of the "Orientation Action Mode" shortcut.

   - Download the "Actions" app for free from the App Store.

4. Customize the "Orientation Action Mode" shortcut to specify the actions you want the action button to perform under various orientations. Here's how:

   - Open the Shortcuts app.

   - Navigate to the "Shortcuts" section at the bottom-left.

   - Locate the "Orientation Action Mode" shortcut and tap the three-dot menu icon at the top-right corner.

Within the shortcut settings, you'll find predefined actions based on device orientation. For instance, when your device is in landscape left orientation, the action button may activate the camera in photo mode. In portrait orientation (the typical vertical holding position), the action button might toggle between silent and ring modes.

However, these are default settings, and you can easily replace them with your preferred actions. To do this:

   - Tap the search bar at the bottom of the shortcut to explore available actions, which may include suggestions based on your installed apps.

   - Choose an action you'd like to assign to the action button, press and hold it, and drag it above the default action. Then, delete the default action to replace it with the new one.

You can assign actions for five different orientations:

   - Landscape right

   - Portrait

   - Landscape left

   - Face up

   - Face down

5. To associate your customized "Orientation Action Mode" shortcut with the action button, follow these steps:

   - Go to "Settings."

- Navigate to "Action Button" and swipe until you reach "Shortcut."

- Select "Choose a Shortcut," and search for "Orientation Action Mode." Choose this shortcut.

6. To activate the "Orientation Action Mode" shortcut and trigger an action, position your device in the desired orientation and hold down the action button.

Please note that the first time you trigger any actions, you may be prompted to grant your phone and the shortcut access to your applications and settings. Simply select "Allow."

You'll know that the "Orientation Action Mode" shortcut is active when it appears in your Dynamic Island.

FACETIME SHAREPLAY FOR SYNCHRONIZED MEDIA SHARING DURING CALLS

FaceTime SharePlay is a revolutionary feature that enables users to share their experiences in the moment with one another. Users are able to share media in a seamless manner while on FaceTime calls, which may be used for a variety of purposes like watching movies, listening to music, and working together on projects. The replay of all participants can be synchronized through the use of SharePlay, which creates an environment for shared viewing or listening. This collaboration function enhances the experience of using FaceTime by allowing users to share in the enjoyment of material together, despite the distance between them. It makes FaceTime into an active platform for shared activities, which helps to build a sense of connection even when people are physically separated.

LINKS TO FACETIME FOR SCHEDULING AND INVITING USERS WHO DON'T HAVE AN APPLE DEVICE TO PARTICIPATE IN FACETIME CALLS

Accessibility and inclusion are both addressed in iOS 17 with the addition of FaceTime links. Users are now able to arrange FaceTime calls in advance, which generates unique links that can be shared with participants in the call. Through these URLs, anyone, regardless of whether or not they have an Apple device, can join FaceTime calls.

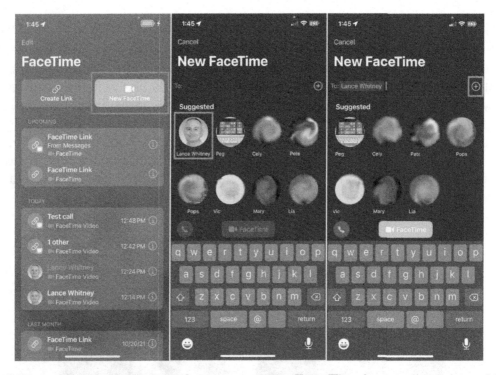

This compatibility with non-Apple platforms expands FaceTime's reach and enables users of Apple and non-Apple devices to communicate with one another in a seamless manner. Through the use of FaceTime links, the process of initiating calls is simplified, making it simpler to connect with loved ones, friends, and coworkers, regardless of the preferred device that each of them uses. This all-encompassing strategy not only expands FaceTime's adaptability but also assures that users may maintain connections with all of the people in their social networks

A QUICK START GUIDE TO THE APP PRIVACY REPORT FOR MONITORING APP BEHAVIOR

The App Privacy Report is a powerful new tool that was introduced in iOS 17 and gives customers valuable insights into the activities of their installed apps. Users are now able to see the frequency with which apps have accessed their private information, including their location, photographs, camera, and microphone, thanks to this new feature. The App Privacy Report delivers a comprehensive summary of how apps behave, ensuring that users are aware of all relevant information and allowing them to make educated choices regarding their personal information. Giving users control over their data and educating them about how applications interact with their devices is a huge step that may be made possible thanks to this openness.

MAIL PRIVACY PROTECTION FOR PREVENTING SENDERS FROM BEING ABLE TO DETERMINE IF AN EMAIL HAS BEEN OPENED

Mail Privacy Protection is a new feature that was introduced in iOS 17 by Apple to improve email privacy. This feature stops senders from knowing when an email has been opened, preventing senders from tracking user activity through read receipts. Senders cannot know when an email has been opened because of this feature. Mail Privacy Protection ensures that user privacy is protected by blocking these tracking pixels, but does so in a way that does not compromise the user's experience with email. When it comes to protecting the privacy of users, particularly in the context of email exchanges, this new feature is an essential component.

ENHANCED PRIVACY SETTINGS AND GREATER TRANSPARENCY REGARDING ACCESS TO LOCATION DATA AND MICROPHONE DATA

iOS 17 places a renewed emphasis on the user's ability to choose how sensitive data is used. The update features improved privacy settings, giving users granular control over which applications can access their location and microphone. The update is available for iOS and Android devices. When an application seeks access to these capabilities, the user is presented with prompts that are both clear and succinct. This ensures that the user is informed of when and how their data is being utilized. Users now have the ability to grant permissions thoughtfully, which improves their overall privacy and security when using a variety of applications thanks to the increased transparency.

Not only do these bolstered privacy features strengthen the user's digital privacy, but they also highlight Apple's commitment to delivering a trustworthy and secure user experience across all of its devices and applications. Users of iOS 17 can confidently explore the digital landscape, knowing that the protection and prioritization of their personal information is a top priority.

CHAPTER THREE
SETTING UP IPHONE 15

Are you thinking about purchasing a snazzy new iPhone 15, possibly one with a titanium finish on the Pro or Pro Max models? The following is a rundown of everything you need to know in order to get it set up.

The Process of Unboxing and Examining the Device

- Unpack the iPhone 15 with caution, making sure there are no signs of damage caused during shipping.

- Examine the product closely for any obvious flaws, scratches, or other types of damage.
- Check to see that all of the supplied equipment, such as the adapter, charging cord, and SIM card ejector tool, are still in their original packaging.
- Make a note of the IMEI and serial number of the device for future reference and in case you need to file a warranty claim.

Accumulating the Required Apparel and Equipment

- Make sure you have the appropriate converter and charging cord for the iPhone 15, which is compatible with that device.

- Finding the SIM card tray ejector tool or using a paperclip to insert the SIM card is necessary if you are using a physical SIM card.
- If you plan to use wireless headphones or other accessories, check to be that they are fully charged and prepared to be paired.
- Establishing a reliable Wi-Fi connection is the first step toward ensuring a smooth setup and transfer of data.

Copying the Information from the Previous Device

- When using iCloud, make sure the older device is attached into a power source and connected to Wi-Fi at the same time.
- Navigate to Settings > [your name] > iCloud > iCloud Backup (if you're using an iOS version older than iOS 14, navigate to iCloud > Backup).
- Activate the iCloud Backup feature, then click "Back Up Now." Attend the conclusion of the backup process.

When using iTunes (on a personal computer), you can

- Launch iTunes once you have it connected to the computer using the USB cable that came with it.
- Choose the icon that looks like your device in iTunes.
- On the Summary tab, locate the Backups section, and select "Back Up Now" from the drop-down menu there. Hold your breath while the backup completes.
- Verify that the backup has been completed by looking at the timestamp for the most recent backup and the state of the backup.
- Proceed to setting up the iPhone 15 once the backup has been validated. During the process of setting up the iPhone 15, you will be able to restore data directly from this backup.

Launching iOS 17 for the Very First Time on the iPhone 15

- The power button can be found on either the right or left side of the iPhone 15, depending on the model. To turn on the device, press and hold the power button until the Apple logo displays on the screen.

- Hold your breath while the equipment starts up. As soon as the device is powered on, the configuration procedure will start.

Choice of Language and Geographic Region:

- Pick your language of choice from the options presented in the drop-down menu.
- Choose your region or country from the list that has been provided.
- Tap the "Continue" button to validate the language and region choices you made.

Establishing an Internet Connection and Connecting to Wireless Networks:

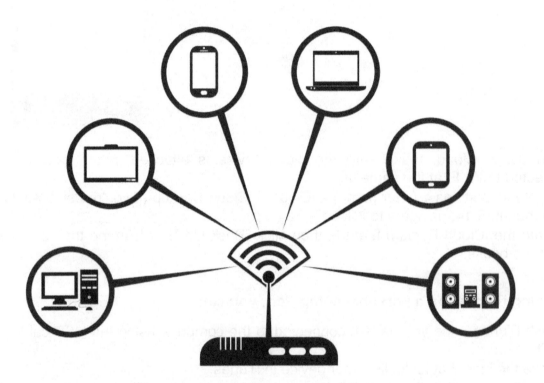

- You will see a list of available Wi-Fi networks when you click that. Choose the Wi-Fi network you want to use.
- If prompted, enter the password for the Wi-Fi network.
- Please be patient as the iPhone 15 attempts to connect to the Wi-Fi network. After you have successfully connected, select "Next" to continue.

Configuring Face ID for the Purposes of Authentication and Security:

- Position your face so that it fits within the on-screen frame, and then move your head slightly to complete the circle. This is required for Face ID.

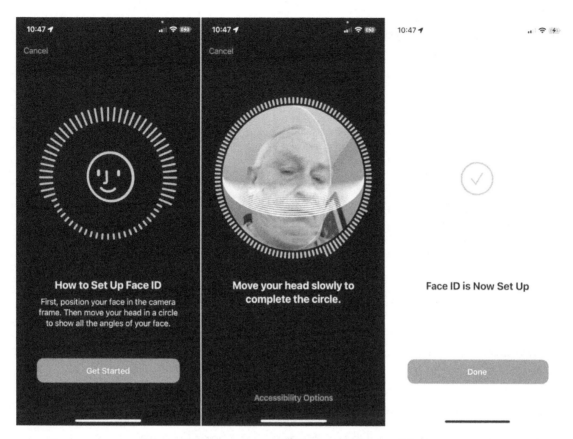

- To move forward once Face ID has been configured, hit the "Continue" button.

Creating a new Apple ID or Signing in with an Existing One

- Tap "Sign In with Your Apple ID" and then input your Apple ID along with its associated password if you already have one.
- Tap the option that says "Don't have an Apple ID or forgot it?" if you do not already have an Apple ID, and then follow the instructions that appear on the screen to set up a new Apple ID.

Enabling or Disabling Services Such as Apple Pay, Siri, and Location Services

- You have the option of turning on Location Services or turning them off. Apps and services can then use your location data for a variety of purposes thanks to this feature.
- Installing Siri is as simple as following the on-screen directions. According to your preferences, you have the option of either activating or deactivating Siri.
- Adjust the settings for Apple Pay, including the addition of credit or debit cards for use in payments and transactions (this step is optional).

Instructions for Configuring Email Accounts in the Mail App

- Launch the Settings app on your iPhone 15 and look under General.
- Scroll all the way down and then select "Mail."
- After selecting "Accounts," select "Add Account."
- Choose your email service provider from the list. Options include Gmail, Outlook, and others.
- After entering your email address and password, simply follow the on-screen directions to finish setting up your account. You could be asked to supply further information, such as the information for your incoming and outgoing mail servers.
- Your email account will be added to the Mail app as soon as the setup is finished, giving you the ability to send and receive emails through your account.

Adding Accounts to Social Media Platforms in Order to Facilitate Integrated Sharing

- Launch the Settings app on your iPhone 15 and look under General.
- You will need to scroll down and then tap on the individual social networking app that you wish to connect (for example, Facebook, Twitter, or Instagram).
- Tap either "Log In" or "Connect Account."
- Please provide your login information (username and password) for the social networking platform.
- Follow the on-screen instructions to grant permission for the app to access your account. It's possible that you'll have to grant permissions before you can publish, make contacts, or use other functions.
- After you have successfully connected, you will have the ability to directly share content from within apps by using the integrated sharing options.

Managing iCloud Settings to Ensure That Your Data Is Synchronized Across Devices

- Launch the Settings app on your iPhone 15 and look under General.
- To access the settings associated with your Apple ID, tap [your name] at the very top of the page.
- To access iCloud, tap the icon.
- In this section, you will find a number of toggles that allow you to enable or disable iCloud synchronization for a variety of apps and data, including Contacts, Calendars, Photos, and more.
- To sync items across all of your devices, activate the switches that are located next to those objects.
- You can access and control your iCloud storage, including backups and app data, by tapping the "Manage Storage" button.
- Go to Settings > [your name] > iCloud > iCloud Backup, and then turn the "iCloud Backup" switch to the "on" position. This will enable iCloud Backup. You can start an instant backup by tapping the "Back Up Now" button on your screen.

When Moving Data from an Android Device to an iOS Device Using the App Called "Move to iOS"

- You can move to iOS by getting the "Move to iOS" app from the Google Play Store and installing it on your Android smartphone.
- After powering on your iPhone 15, navigate through the basic setup wizard until you reach the "Apps & Data" section.
- Click the option labeled "Move Data from Android." On the screen of your iPhone, a code of between six and ten digits will appear.
- On your Android device, launch the "Move to iOS" application, and then select "Continue."
- Please take the time to read and acknowledge the terms and conditions. To proceed, select "Next."
- On your iPhone, a code of between six and ten digits will appear; enter that code into your Android device.
- After you have successfully linked your devices, choose the kinds of data you wish to transfer (for example, contacts, message history, images, videos, bookmarks on websites, and so on).
- Attend until the process of the transfer is finished. The amount of data being sent has an effect on how long it takes to complete.
- Once the file transmission is finished, you can access the "Done" button on your Android device.
- To complete the setup procedure on your iPhone, select "Continue Setting Up iPhone" from the Settings menu.

Checking the Data That Has Been Transferred and Making Sure It Is Correct

- Examine the information that has been moved to your iPhone 15, including your contacts, messages, photos, and videos.
- Check the integrity of the data stored in certain applications, especially if you have moved app data between devices.
- Check to see that all of your multimedia files, such as images and movies, are complete and can be accessed easily.
- Verify that all of your contacts, messages, and call records have been moved correctly.
- Apps that have been moved should be tested to ensure that they retain their original functionality and contain all of the essential data.
- In the event that inconsistencies are discovered, it may be necessary to retransfer the data via the "Move to iOS" software or to transfer certain data manually, depending on the circumstances.

CHAPTER FOUR
HOW TO SET UP APPLE PAY

Getting started with Apple Pay is an easy step to go through. Using your iPhone, iPad, Apple Watch, or Mac in conjunction with Apple Pay enables you to make safe and secure transactions in-store, within apps, and on websites. Activating Apple Pay on your iPhone can be done in the following ways

INTRODUCTION TO APPLE PAY AND ITS BENEFIT

Apple Pay is a game-changing mobile payment system as well as a digital wallet service that was developed by Apple Inc. It enables customers to make safe, contactless payments using their Apple devices, such as their iPhone, iPad, Apple Watch, and Mac computers. These purchases may be made in stores, within apps, and on websites. The following is a rundown of its most important characteristics and advantages:

Payments That Are Both Convenient And Quick Apple Pay Simplifies The Payment Process By Allowing Users To Complete Transactions With The Tap Of Their Device It Also Makes Payments More Convenient And Faster. Because of this, there is no longer a requirement to carry around real wallets or currency, which makes conducting transactions in everyday life more quicker and less cumbersome.

Safe and Confidential: Apple Pay puts the safety and discretion of its customers first. When a card is added to Apple Pay, the actual card numbers are not saved on the device or on Apple's servers. This is the case even if the card is stored locally on the device. In its place, the device's Secure Element is given a one-of-a-kind Device Account Number, which is then encrypted before being safely kept there. This assures that all private and financial information is kept in strict confidence.

Contactless Payments: Apple Pay makes use of technology known as Near Field Communication (NFC), which enables customers to make contactless payments at retail terminals that are compatible with the service. Face ID, Touch ID, or a passcode can be used to validate the transaction if the user merely holds their iPhone or Apple Watch up to the payment terminal. Alternatively, the user can enter a passcode.

Apple Pay Enables Secure Transactions Within Apps and Online Apple Pay enables users to conduct secure transactions within apps and on websites. Customers are able to make transactions without having to manually enter their card details, which lowers the likelihood of a data breach occurring. The process of checking out is streamlined thanks to this function, which also improves the whole experience of purchasing online.

STEP BY STEP GUIDE TO ADDING CREDIT/DEBIT CARDS

The procedure of adding a credit or debit card to Apple Pay is a simple one that ensures your payment information is saved safely on your device. The following is a guide that will walk you through the process of adding your cards to Apple Pay:

1. Launch the Wallet application.

Start the Wallet app on your iOS device, be it an iPhone or an iPad. You can get the app from the App Store if you don't already have it on your device.

2. Select "Add Credit or Debit Card" by tapping on it:

Tap the "+" button within the Wallet app. This icon is typically found in the upper right corner of the screen. After that, choose the option that says "Credit or Debit Card."

3. Arrange Your Greeting Card Within the Frame:

The camera on your device will then open. Put your credit card or debit card into the frame that's been supplied. When you use Apple Pay, the card number and expiration date will be retrieved automatically. You also have the option of selecting the "Enter Card Details Manually" option and entering the information by hand.

4. Check the Information on the Card:

Apple Pay may ask you to verify additional information such as the card's security code after you have scanned or entered the card details. This may happen regardless of whether you scanned or entered the card details. Please enter the needed information to proceed.

5. Confirm that you accept the Terms and Conditions:

When you use Apple Pay, you will be shown the terms and restrictions associated with its use. After reading everything, select "Agree" to move forward.

6. Make Sure You're Who You Say You Are:

Depending on the financial institution you use, you might be asked to provide identity documentation. This can be accomplished through the use of a verification code that is either emailed, texted, or given over the phone. When prompted, enter the code in question.

7. The Card Verification Process Has Been Finished:

After the completion of the identity verification process, your credit or debit card will be connected to Apple Pay successfully. You can use it to make purchases in-app, online, and in stores as of right now.

8. Set a Default Card

If you add more than one card, you will have the option to select which one will be used for transactions by default. Tap the card in the Wallet app that you wish to use as the default, scroll down, and then select "Set as Default Card."

9. Add Credit Cards to Your Apple Watch and Mac (If Necessary):

If you have an Apple Watch, you can add a credit or debit card to Apple Pay by opening the Apple Watch app on your iPhone, selecting "Wallet & Apple Pay," then selecting "Add Credit or Debit Card" and following the on-screen directions. To add a card using Apple Pay on a Mac, navigate to System Preferences > Wallet & Apple Pay, click the "Add Card" button, and then follow the on-screen instructions.

HOW TO MAKE PAYMENTS IN PHYSICAL STORES USING IPHONE AND APPLE WATCH

When making purchases in-store, using Apple Pay is a speedy, risk-free, and simple option. Here's how you can use your iPhone or Apple Watch to make payments inside traditional brick-and-mortar establishments:

While using an iPhone:

1. Reanimate Your Sleeping iPhone:

To bring your sleeping iPhone back to life, click either the Side button (available on iPhone X and later models) or the Home button (available on iPhone 8 and older models). When you glance at your smartphone with your face in front of it, if it has Face ID, it will immediately recognize your face.

2. Verify your identity using either Face ID or Touch ID:

Place your finger on the Touch ID sensor of your iPhone when it is in close proximity to the contactless payment scanner. If your iPhone is equipped with Face ID, look at your iPhone instead. This confirms the payment and establishes that you are who you say you are.

3. Finalize the Business Transaction

After you have been shown to be who you say you are, the money will be processed, and a confirmation will appear on your screen. There is also a possibility that you will feel a slight vibration, which will confirm that the payment was successful.

When use an Apple Watch:

1. Double-click the button located on the side:

Double-clicking the side button (the smaller button below the Digital Crown) of your Apple Watch in rapid succession enables Apple Pay to be used on your device.

2. Keep an Eye on Your Watch While You're Near the Cash Register:

Keep the screen of your Apple Watch within close proximity to the contactless payment scanner. Check that the watch is aligned properly and that the display is towards the person who is reading it.

3. Be Patient and Await Confirmation:

You will know that the process is complete when you feel a light tap on your wrist and the word "Done" appears on the face of the watch. This suggests that the money was processed without any problems.

Advice to Help Make the Deal Go Smoothly:

- Make Sure Your Device or Watch Is Near the Reader In order for the transaction to go through successfully, you will need to ensure that your iPhone or Apple Watch is within a few inches of the contactless payment reader.
- Set Up Face ID or Touch ID: If you have an iPhone with Face ID, you need to make sure that it is configured properly and that it is enabled for Apple Pay. Make sure that your fingerprints are recorded on any iPhones that have the Touch ID feature. Check that your Apple Watch has a passcode by setting it up.
- Look for the Apple Pay Logo: When you are at the store's payment terminal, you should look for the Apple Pay logo or the contactless payment symbol. This will let you know that the store accepts Apple Pay.
- Follow the Instructions Displayed on the Screen In order to successfully complete the transaction, the payment terminal may require extra steps, such as entering a PIN. In this case, it is important to follow the instructions displayed on the screen.

TTIPS FOR MAXIMIMIZING BENEFITS AND REWARDS WITH APPLE PAYS

- Include Loyalty Programs as well as Reward Cards:
- You can include any reward cards, loyalty programs, or membership cards you already have into the Wallet app. You will be able to receive points, discounts, and cashback for purchases that you make with Apple Pay thanks to this feature.
- Look into the Unique Deals and Discounts That Are Available:
  Keep an eye out for limited-time deals and savings opportunities made available by stores, banks, and credit card issuers. Using Apple Pay can get you access to special discounts and deals from a variety of retailers, which can result in significant savings on your purchases.
- Make Use of Credit Cards That Offer Cash Back:
  Integrate credit cards that offer cashback rewards with your Apple Pay account. You will earn cashback rewards whenever you make a purchase with Apple Pay. These points can be accumulated over time and then redeemed for a variety of other perks.
- Take part in the Apple Card Rewards program:
  When you make a purchase with Apple Pay and have an Apple Card, you can earn daily cashback on the amount of the purchase. This cashback can be spent immediately, saved for later use, or transferred to the balance on your Apple Card, providing you with flexibility in the way that you use your rewards.
- Use Apple Pay to make purchases in apps and online stores:
  Apple Pay should be the payment method of choice whether you are making purchases within applications or online. During the checkout process, many online businesses and services provide customers with access to special savings or cashback incentives if they use Apple Pay.
- Keep an eye out for partner apps and promotions:
  When you use Apple Pay with certain partner applications and services, you can earn additional incentives. If you use Apple Pay, you should check the terms and conditions of a

variety of apps and services to see if they give any additional perks to customers who use Apple Pay.

- Keep Up to Date on the Latest Promotions:
  Maintain an up-to-date awareness of the latest announcements and deals made available by Apple and your banking institutions. These businesses frequently host limited-time promotions or one-time-only events that give you the opportunity to earn additional points for making purchases with Apple Pay.
- Integrate Apple Pay with Other Loyalty Programs:
- You are able to stack rewards with some credit cards and customer loyalty programs. If you use Apple Pay in conjunction with these programs, you can increase the number of rewards you receive by earning points or cashback from both your credit card company and the particular retailer or service you use.

HOW TO CONFIRM IDENTITY FOR APPLE PAY

Launch the Wallet application:

Start the Wallet app on your iOS device, be it an iPhone or an iPad. You will be asked to set up Apple Pay if you haven't done so already if you haven't already.

To use Apple Pay open the Wallet app and then select the Apple Pay option from the menu. In the event that you have not yet contributed any cards, you will be prompted to do so.

Follow the on-screen instructions to add your credit or debit card by clicking the "Add a Card" button. You have the option of entering the card information manually or using the camera to automatically gather the information from the card.

After adding your card, the bank that is affiliated with your card will need to validate your identification before continuing with the verification process. The procedure for verifying your identity could be different depending on the requirements of your bank, however it typically requires one of the following methods:

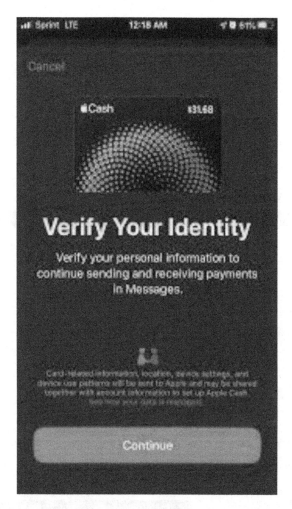

Verification through SMS:

It is possible that you will receive a verification code via SMS. To verify your identity during the setup process for Apple Pay, enter this verification code.

Email Verification

In certain instances, the verification code could be delivered to the email address that is connected to the bank account that you have. Check your email for the code, then retrieve it and input it into the Apple Pay setup when prompted.

A phone call from your bank could come as part of the identification verification process. They might verify your identification by interrogating you with a few standard security questions.

Verification in Person:

Depending on your bank and the region in which you live, you may be required to make a personal appearance at your bank as part of the verification procedure.

Completion and Utilization: Once Apple has determined that you are who you say you are, your credit card will be added to Apple Pay, and you will then be able to use it to make payments in stores, applications, and online.

CHAPTER FIVE
EXPLORE THE APP STORE

Exploring apps has become vital in the digital age. The process of delving into the complexities of a software program to comprehend its features, functionalities, and prospective applications is referred to as app exploration. This research is critical in a world dominated by technology because it enables users to leverage the full potential of programs, maximizing their utility and providing a seamless user experience.

Overview of the User Interface

Understanding an app's interface is the first step toward mastering it. Users will delve into the application's visual characteristics here, learning about the positioning of menus, buttons, and interactive elements. Users will learn to understand the purpose of each element through extensive descriptions and graphical representations, facilitating efficient navigation. Understanding the logic behind the layout boosts user confidence, resulting in a more fluid and intuitive engagement with the app.

The user interface's key features, such as home screens, menus, and toolbars, are dissected for easy comprehension.

Visual signals such as icons and color schemes are described, assisting users in quickly identifying functions.

Interactive walkthroughs and lessons are provided to enhance comprehension and ensure users effectively comprehend the interface intricacies.

Key Features and Customization Possibilities

This section digs deeper into the app's basic features and the different ways users can tailor their experience. Users obtain a thorough understanding of the app's capabilities by thoroughly investigating its operations, allowing them to use it to its maximum potential.

Exploration of Core Features: Users are introduced to the essential features that define the app's purpose. Each feature is examined in depth, stressing its importance in the user experience, whether it be communications, content creation, or data analysis.

Beyond the fundamentals, users are taken through the app's deeper features. This includes capabilities for collaboration, data sharing, and integration with other apps. Understanding these advanced features enables users to enhance their process and achieve their goals.

Mastery of Customization: Users are educated on the art of customisation. This section takes users through the process of customizing the app to meet their specific needs, from theme selection to designing custom workflows. Users can transform the app into a personalized tool by exploring customization possibilities, increasing both efficiency and user pleasure.

Users obtain a full grasp of the app's design, functionalities, and customization choices through this in-depth investigation. Armed with this knowledge, customers can confidently browse the app, fully utilize its capabilities, and customise it to their individual needs, ensuring a tailored and fulfilling user experience.

Sections and Multimedia Access

Understanding how to access different parts and explore multimedia features effectively is required when navigating the content of an app. This section walks users through the procedures necessary to access various areas of the app and interact with multimedia content.

Section Access: Users learn how to navigate the app's sections, categories, and tabs. Users can quickly browse to topics of interest thanks to clear instructions.

Understanding multimedia content such as photos, movies, and music is critical for multimedia interaction. Users learn how to view, play, and interact with multimedia elements within the app, resulting in a rich and engaging experience.

Organizational Structure and Available Search Methods

Efficient exploration necessitates an understanding of the app's organizational system and search capabilities. This section explains how the app's data is organized and how users may search for specific material efficiently.

Organizational Hierarchy: Users receive knowledge of the app's hierarchical structure, such as folders, collections, or categorization methods. Understanding how data is arranged enables consumers to quickly locate specific information.

Search Functionality: It is critical to master the search choices. Users are taught how to use search filters, keywords, and sophisticated search options to swiftly find specific content. There are tips and tactics provided to improve search accuracy and relevancy.

Users are armed with the skills needed to explore the app's content efficiently and meaningfully by thoroughly covering the access methods for sections and multimedia, as well as unraveling the app's organizational structure and search choices. This expertise guarantees that users can quickly find what they're looking for and effortlessly interact with the app's multimedia offerings.

User Interaction and Social Features

Interacting with an app entails more than just navigation; it entails active interaction and comprehension of its social functionalities. This section introduces users to the app's interactive aspects, which build friendships and social interactions on the platform.

User Engagement Tools: Users learn how to interact with material by doing things like liking, commenting, and sharing. Polls and quizzes are examples of interactive elements that increase user participation.

Understanding social elements such as friend requests, follower procedures, and private messaging is critical. This information allows users to connect with others, creating a sense of community within the app.

Troubleshooting and Frequently Asked Questions

No app exploration is complete unless common difficulties and user inquiries are addressed. This area provides users with troubleshooting tools and answers to frequently asked questions, guaranteeing a positive user experience.

Common difficulties Resolution: Users are directed through the process of resolving common difficulties such as error messages, sluggish performance, and login issues. To properly fix these issues, step-by-step solutions are presented.

Questions and Answers (FAQs): A selected selection of FAQs provides thorough answers to user questions. These FAQs include subjects ranging from fundamental functionality to complex capabilities, allowing users to quickly discover answers to their questions.

Data Security Procedures

Users are presented to the app's robust security protocols, which are designed to protect user data. There are detailed descriptions of encryption mechanisms, secure data transport, and secure storage practices. Users obtain visibility into how their information is encrypted during transmission, ensuring that it remains indecipherable to unauthorized parties even if intercepted. The section looks into secure storage procedures, emphasizing how user data is encrypted and stored in an encrypted way to improve protection against unauthorized access.

- Encryption Protocols: Users learn about the app's encryption techniques, as well as the complicated codes that secure their data from unauthorized access. Extensive examples explain how encryption works, demystifying the technology for people.
- Secure Data Transmission: This section explains the secure sockets layer (SSL) and transport layer security (TLS) technologies. Users understand how these protocols create secure communication channels, preventing eavesdropping and data tampering while in transit.
- Secure Storage Practices: Users investigate how their data is securely stored on the app's servers. Encryption at rest is explained, detailing how data remains encrypted when stored, ensuring that data remains inaccessible even if physical servers are compromised.

Mastery of Privacy Settings

Within the app, this feature allows users to take control of their digital presence. Users are directed through the app's privacy settings, allowing them to tailor their experience to their preferences.

- Profile Visibility: Users learn how to control who can see the information on their profiles. They can change the settings to limit visibility to specific user groups, ensuring that only trusted connections have access to their personal information.

- Data Access Control: Users learn how to manage third-party applications and services that may access their data. There are detailed instructions for cancelling access, judiciously providing rights, and monitoring app integrations.
- Interaction Privacy: Users can control who can send messages, comments, or friend requests by exploring options connected to interactions. This level of control ensures that users can participate in a relaxed manner, eliminating unwanted contacts and promoting genuine connections.

ITUNES

A media player, a media library, an online radio broadcaster, and a mobile device management tool, iTunes was developed and distributed by Apple Inc. It served as a hub for managing and playing digital music and video files on both Mac and Windows PCs, and it was compatible with both operating systems. Users were able to use iTunes to purchase and download music, movies, television series, audiobooks, and podcasts, as well as to organize their collections of these media. In addition to that, it included alternatives for transferring content between iPods, iPhones, and iPads.

Users had the ability to utilize iTunes to create playlists, burn CDs, as well as buy and download a broad variety of multimedia items from the iTunes shop, which is Apple's online digital media shop. In addition, iTunes offered features such as Genius playlists, which created playlists based on the users' selections of music, and Home Sharing, which enabled users to share their iTunes collections with other devices that were connected to the same network. Genius playlists and Home Sharing were both available to users.

Please keep in mind that as of my most recent update in September 2021, iTunes has been discontinued, and its functionality has been separated into several new applications. These apps include Apple Music for streaming music, Apple TV for watching movies and television shows, and Apple Podcasts for listening to podcasts. Users of Mac computers have the ability to operate their machines by using the Finder application. If you are looking for the most up-to-date information, it is highly advised that you check out Apple's official materials or website.

HOW TO AUTOMATE AND PROGRAM FOCUS MODES

Productivity and digital well-being can be dramatically improved by using automation and programming to program attention modes across different devices and operating systems. The device and operating system both have a role in determining the exact methods that are available for automating and programming focus modes.

I'll provide an overview of the general instructions for the most common platforms below:

Using Shortcuts to Automate Focus Modes on iOS/iPadOS:

Make a shortcut:

- On your iOS/iPadOS device, launch the Shortcuts app.
- To make a new shortcut, tap the "+" icon.
- Create actions for the shortcut. You can, for example, change the focus mode, adjust the volume, or start specific apps.

Shortcut Automation:

- On the upper right of your shortcut, tap the three dots (ellipsis).
- Select "Automation."
- To create a new automation, tap the "+" icon.
- Select a trigger for your automation (for example, Time of Day, Arrive at Location).
- Configure the trigger settings.
- Add the previously created shortcut to the automation.

THE SETTING APP

Configure the trigger settings.

Add the previously created shortcut to the automation.

Now, the focus mode will activate automatically based on the conditions you set in your automation.

You appear to be referring to the Settings app, which is a key component of most modern operating systems such as iOS, iPadOS, Android, and Windows. Users can utilize the Settings app to change numerous aspects of their smartphone, such as network settings, security and privacy settings, app preferences, and more. I'll give you a general overview of how to utilize the Settings app on various platforms below:

iPadOS and iOS:

The Settings app on iOS and iPadOS looks like a gear symbol. Tap on the icon on your home screen to get there. Wi-Fi, Bluetooth, Display & Brightness, and many other categories may be found within the Settings app.

How to Use the Settings App:

- Once inside the Settings app, you may personalize your device by navigating through several categories. Here are some examples of frequent categories:
- Wireless & Networks: Set up Wi-Fi, mobile data, and Bluetooth.
- Adjust the screen brightness, background, sound volume, and notification sounds.
- Apps: Control installed apps, permissions, and notifications.
- Set up screen lock, fingerprint or Face ID (on supported smartphones), and control app permissions for security and privacy.

- Accounts: Add or remove email, social networking, and other service accounts.
- System: Change system settings, update your device, and gain access to accessibility features.

THE APP STORE

The App Store is a digital distribution platform that allows users to purchase and download mobile applications for use on iOS-based devices (such as iPhones and iPads) as well as desktops running macOS. As the official platform for downloading and installing programs for Apple devices, it is run and maintained by Apple Inc., which also serves as the platform's administrator.

The App Store gives developers the opportunity to distribute their software to a large number of users of Apple's iOS and macOS operating systems. Users are able to search for, browse, and download applications directly from the store onto their own devices.

CHAPTER SIX:
HOW TO FORCE CLOSE ACTIVE APPLICATIONS ON IPHONE 15 FROM THE APP SWITCHER

You can force close active programs using the App Switcher on the iPhone 13 and other iPhones that have Face ID by following these steps:

Get in touch with the App Switcher:

Swipe up from the bottom edge of the screen on an iPhone 13 and pause in the middle of the screen. This step will bring up the App Switcher, which will display all of the apps that are currently open on your device.

Look at the Running Programs:

You will be able to view all of the applications that are now operating in the background as little app cards within the App Switcher.

Put pressure on Put an app to rest:

Swipe to the left or right to move through the active app cards until you find the app that you want to force close and then tap it to close it.

Put pressure on Put an end to the app:

When you have found the app that you want to quit, swipe the app card up and off the top of the screen to exit the app. This action will close the app in an unnatural way.

Please take note that forcibly closing apps is not typically required in order to effectively manage the performance of your device or the battery life of its battery. The Apple iOS was created to manage applications in the most effective manner possible, and the system will automatically put applications into a suspended state if they are not being actively utilized. However, if an application is not responding properly or is broken, dismissing it with the force button can be helpful.

HOW TO CHANGE CAMERA SETTING?

Open the application that deals with the Camera:

You can launch the Camera app by selecting the Camera icon that appears on the home screen. It looks like the lens from a camera and has the same shape.

You can change the settings of the camera by accessing:

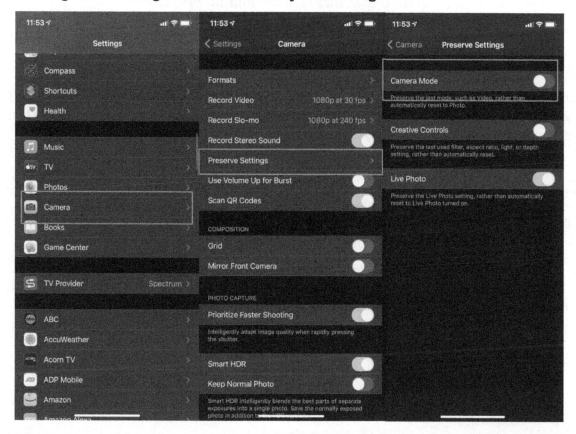

After you have opened the Camera app, you will need to find the symbol that looks like a gear and choose it. It often takes the shape of a gear and can be located at either the top or bottom of the screen, depending on the orientation of the device that you are using.

Make Changes to Some of the Default Settings:

Tap the icon that looks like a gear to access the core camera choices, such as HDR (High Dynamic Range), Flash, Live Photo, and Timer. You can also access these options by holding down the shutter button. You have the power to toggle the visibility of these settings on or off, according to your own preferences.

Gain Access to Further Configuration Options:

Additional camera modes and options can be accessed by swiping up or down on the screen (or left on the iPhone 13 series), respectively. You can use the iPhone 13 series if the settings require greater sophistication.

You may or may not see options such as Night mode, Portrait mode, and Panorama mode. There is a possibility that you will. You have the ability to make individual adjustments to the settings for each mode.

You can access additional settings that are unique to a certain mode by tapping on that mode, such as the Portrait mode. These settings are not available in any other mode. The camera's Portrait mode, for instance, enables users to exercise control over the various lighting effects.

Changing the Settings (provided that this is an available option):

On some iPhone models, particularly newer ones, you have the ability to make granular modifications to various parameters within each camera mode. This is especially true of newer models.

If you want to access other options when you are in a certain mode, check for icons like () or (v). These will give you access to those settings. When you are in the Photo mode, for instance, you can alter the settings for exposure, focus, and white balance by utilizing these symbols.

Utilize the Settings app in order to make any and all global settings to your camera:

By opening the main Settings app on your iPhone and navigating to the Camera section, you will be able to access global camera settings such as grid, formats, and preserve settings.

To use the camera, scroll all the way down to the bottom of the page, then click the "Camera" button. In this part, you will discover a number of settings that may be customized, such as the Grid, the ability to scan QR codes, and the recording of videos.

CHAPTER SEVEN:
APPLE ID AND ICLOUD

The Apple ID is composed of:

When a user logs in using their Apple ID, they are able to access a wide range of Apple services, including the App Store, iCloud, and Apple Music, amongst others. A single person can only have one Apple ID at a time.

This is significant because it works as a portal to Apple's ecosystem, making it possible for Apple's many devices to integrate with one another in a seamless manner, providing secure access to applications, and enabling users to have individualized experiences.

This is the iCloud:

Apple's iCloud is a cloud-based storage and computing service that enables users to preserve data, including as images, videos, documents, and app backups, in a safe and secure manner within the cloud. Users may access this material from any internet-connected device, such as a computer, smartphone, or tablet.

Importance: It ensures data synchronization between devices, makes it possible to do automatic backups, and provides a platform for seamless collaboration and sharing, all of which contribute to an increase in both the user's convenience and the data's level of security.

CREATION AND MANAGEMENT

In order to create an Apple ID:

Creating an Apple ID is required in order to access a wide variety of services and content that are exclusive to Apple devices. This is the procedure to follow:

Visit the Apple website or make use of an Apple device in order to:

Go to the Apple website or use an Apple device and navigate to Settings > Sign in to your iPhone (or iPad, iPod Touch, or Mac). You may also do this on an Apple computer.

Make the Necessary Information Available:

You are going to be asked for many pieces of information, including your email address, password, and possibly some security questions. It is essential to make use of a current email address that you check on a regular basis.

Please Check Your Email:

Apple will verify the entered email address by sending a verification email to that address. To verify your account, please follow the link that was provided in the email.

Put in Place Safety Precautions:

To increase the level of protection provided, turn on two-factor authentication. This makes it so that even if someone has your password, they still won't be able to access your account unless they also provide a second form of authentication.

You can customize your account by:

Include a photo of yourself in your profile, and fill out your personal information. This step is completely voluntary but will improve your overall Apple experience.

Once you have an Apple ID, you may use it to log in to a variety of Apple services, including the following:

The App Store:

In order to download applications, games, and other content from the App Store, you will need to sign in with your Apple ID.

The iCloud:

Use iCloud to store your photographs, movies, and documents, as well as backups of your various devices, in a safe manner. It ensures that your various Apple devices are perfectly synchronized with one another.

Itunes: Apple Music

Simply sign in with your Apple ID to access Apple Music's extensive music catalog and start listening right away. You are able to make playlists, discover new artists, and even download songs to listen to while you are not connected to the internet.

Pay with Apple:

Connect your debit or credit card to your Apple ID, and then use Apple Pay to conduct transactions that are safe and convenient, whether you're shopping online or in a physical store.

The iTunes Store and the Apple TV:

By logging in to iTunes and Apple TV with your Apple ID, you will have access to a wide variety of media, including movies, television series, and podcasts.

The Importance of:

- Continuity of Experience Across Devices Using your Apple ID to sign in to services guarantees that your experience is consistent from one device to the next. You are able to begin performing an activity on one device and then seamlessly continue it on another device without missing a beat.
- Synchronization of Data: If you use iCloud, your images, documents, and the data from your apps will all be synchronized. This will ensure that you always have access to the information that is most essential to you.
- Protection: Apple ID provides comprehensive security features, like as two-factor authentication, to safeguard both your account and your personal information.
- Personalization: Your Apple ID gives you the ability to customize your devices, services, and content, making it possible to create a digital experience that is unique to your tastes and preferences.

ICLOUD'S STORAGE PLANS AND ADMINISTRATIVE CONTROLS

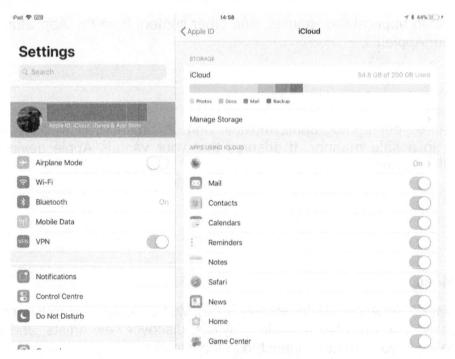

iCloud provides users with a variety of storage plan options to accommodate their individual requirements. The following is a comprehensive look at the different iCloud storage plans and how to manage your account:

Plans and Capacity Options for Currently Available Storage:

Free Space for Storing:

Apple gives each customer a free storage space of 5 gigabytes in the iCloud to utilize.

This space is adequate for meeting fundamental requirements such as making backups of electronic devices and storing some photographs and papers.

Storage Plans That Require Payment:

Apple has premium plans with increased storage capacities, including the following:

- The 50 GB plan is perfect for users that require a greater amount of space for their data.
- The 200 GB Plan is ideal for those who need a substantial amount of data storage, such as families or businesses.
- The 2 TB plan is ideal for power users, families, or individuals with extensive data usage, such as persons with large media collections or large media libraries.

Managing and Increasing Your iCloud Storage Capacity:

Increasing the Capacity of Your iCloud Storage Plan:

- Navigate to Settings > [Your Name] > iCloud > Manage Storage on your iOS or iPadOS device.
- Select the desired storage plan by tapping the "Change Storage Plan" button.
- To finish the payment procedure, just follow the on-screen prompts.
- Using a Mac
- Select System Preferences > Apple ID > iCloud, and then select Manage from the drop-down box.
- Choose the storage plan you want by clicking the "Change Storage Plan" button.
- In order to finish the upgrade, you will need to confirm the password for your Apple ID.

Managing Storage in the iCloud:

Examining the Current Use:

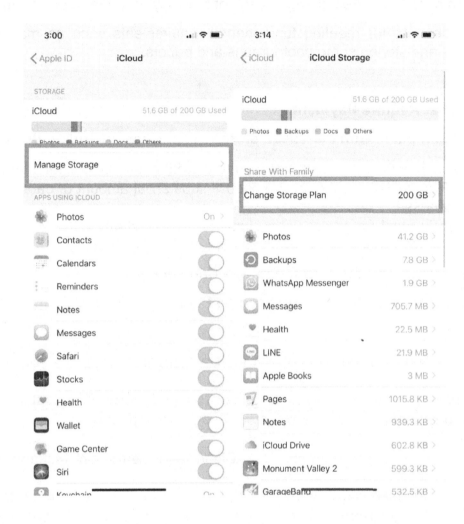

To view how your storage is being utilized, go to System Preferences > Apple ID > iCloud > Manage (on a Mac) or Settings > [Your Name] > iCloud > Manage Storage (on iOS/iPadOS).

Enabling "Optimize iPhone Storage" (on iOS/iPadOS) or "Optimize Mac Storage" (on Mac) will allow you to store full-resolution photographs and videos in iCloud while keeping just smaller copies on your device, so saving local storage. These options are found under "Optimize Storage" in the respective operating system menus.

Getting Rid of Old Backups and Files to make more room in your iCloud storage, delete any old backups of your devices as well as any files that aren't needed. To erase certain files, go to Manage Storage, pick a backup or an app, and then press "Delete Data" or "Delete Documents & Data."

Family Sharing: If you have an iCloud storage plan that includes family sharing, your iCloud storage can be shared with other members of your family, making it a more cost-effective choice for numerous users.

The Advantages of an Effectively Managed iCloud Storage Account:

The Accessibility and Safety of the Data:

By creating backups of critical files and documents, you can ensure that your data is safe at all times.

Provides access to your stored information from any Apple device that is synced with your iCloud account.

Upgrades to Devices That Cause No Downtime:

The process of upgrading to a new device is made easier by this feature. You can ensure that all of your apps and data are carried over to your new device without any difficulty by restoring it from an iCloud backup.

Management of Photographs and Videos:

Manages your photo and video library, giving you the ability to save, view, and share multimedia information across all of your devices in a seamless manner.

Effective Application Use:

Your app's data will be optimized, ensuring that your apps run smoothly without using an excessive amount of your local storage space.

IMPORTANCE OF APPLE ID AND ICLOUDS

Within the Apple ecosystem, the Apple ID and iCloud both play critical roles in boosting consumer ease, security, and the ability to personalize their experience. These services serve as the pillars around which Apple's networked products are built, and they foster a digital experience that is cohesive and friendly to users.

Apple ID & iCloud

In their most fundamental form, Apple ID and iCloud are not only services; rather, they represent the fundamental building blocks of the Apple ecosystem. Users are able to feel respected, protected, and empowered in an atmosphere that was created by the seamless integration, emphasis on security, and focus on personalization of these features. As a consequence of this, customers are more likely to remain faithful to Apple, which helps to cultivate a solid and long-lasting relationship between the firm and its clientele.

ALL ABOUT HOME SCREEN PAGE AND HOW TO SET THEM

What exactly are those pages on the home screen?

When you scroll to the left or right on the Home Screen of your iPhone or iPad, you will see various pages that each display a different selection of apps. This is where all of your apps can be found. The search bar and a list of widgets may be found on the extreme left side of the interface, and the iPhone or iPad App Library can be found on the extreme right. However, all of those screens in the middle represent the sites on your Home Screen.

Instructions for Adding New Pages to the Home Screen on an iPhone or iPad

It won't take you more than a few clicks to add a new page to your Home Screen, despite how simple the process may seem. Simply proceed in the following manner:

- You can make your Home Screen jiggle by pressing and holding any app on your Home Screen until it does so.
- You can create a new page for the app you want by dragging it to the right side of the screen.
- Keep moving the app to the right until you reach the page that is the last one before the App Library.
- To quit Jiggle mode, just drop the app on the new page and tap anywhere on the screen.

How to Rearrange the Pages on Your Home Screen on an iPhone or iPad

It is also possible to rearrange the pages on your Home Screen so that they are in the order that you prefer to see them in. Don't worry; it's as simple as reorganizing your programs to fix the problem. This is the procedure to follow:

- Keep pressing and holding an empty place on the Home Screen until the icons of the apps begin to move about.
- If you want to see an overview of your pages, tap the dots that are near the bottom of your screen.
- Maintain pressure on the page you wish to move, and then release it.
- First, move the page to the location where you want it to be, and then let go of it.
- Tap the Done button in the upper-right hand corner of your screen when you are completed.

How to Hide Pages on Your Home Screen on an iPhone or iPad

  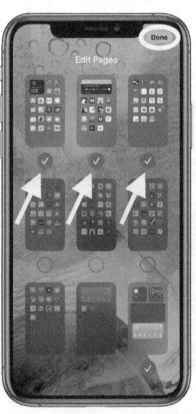

The fact that Home Screen pages can be made invisible at any time is one of their many appealing features. This enables you to streamline your Home Screen by concealing any and all pages that you do not frequently access. Alternately, you may use it to hide particular pages until you require them at different times of the day, which is something that we will demonstrate how to automate for you later on.

To begin, however, here is how you can manually hide a page from the Home Screen:

- Keep pressing and holding an empty place on the Home Screen until the icons of the apps begin to move about.
- Tap the dots that are located close to the bottom of the screen.
- Simply tapping the circle at the bottom of the page will clear the checkmark.

- When you are finished, select Done from the menu that appears in the upper right corner of your screen.

HOW TO TAKE SCREENSHOT

The first step is to:

The first step is to navigate to the screen on your Apple iPhone 15 Plus that you wish to take a screenshot of. This may be a web page, a chat window, or an application screen.

The second step is to turn on your iPhone 15 Plus by simultaneously pressing the power button and the volume up button. Quickly let go of both of the buttons.

In the third phase, the image that has been captured will be shrunk down and will temporarily appear in the bottom-left corner of the screen on the iPhone 15 Plus.

If you want to alter the capture right away or share it with others, you'll need to click on the thumbnail before it disappears. You are free to ignore the thumbnail and carry on using the device as normal if you do not intend to make use of the screenshot at this time. If necessary, you can take further screenshots.

In the fourth step, if you have selected the thumbnail by clicking on it, the editor for the screenshot will open and you will be able to make changes to it. You have the option of chopping it up, drawing on it, erasing portions of it, adding arrows, circles, remark boxes, using the magnifying glass, adding text, or signing it. Before you show the screenshot to other people, you might find it helpful to annotate it with notes or highlight relevant information using one of these tools.

The fifth step is to tap the "OK" button once you have completed modifying the capture so that it can be saved in the photo gallery of your iPhone 15 Plus. You will be presented with a confirmation popup that gives you the option to either save the screenshot to your photo album or delete it.

HOW TO USE SAFARI TO BROWSE THE WEB

Configure the trigger settings.
Add the previously created shortcut to the automation.
Now, the focus mode will activate automatically based on the conditions you set in your automation.

Open Safari on your iPhone or iPad:
On your home screen, tap the Safari icon.

Go to the following website:
At the top, tap the address bar.
Enter a URL or a search keyword.
Click "Go" to get to the website.

Browsing:
To scroll, swipe up/down.

To zoom, pinch in and out.
Open links by tapping them.
For several websites, use tabs.
Bookmarks and Social Sharing:
To save sites, tap the bookmarks icon.
To send or save web pages, click the share icon.
On Mac:

Launch Safari:
In the Dock or Applications folder, select the Safari icon.
Go to the following website:
At the top, click the address bar.
Enter a URL or a search keyword.
Click "Return" to return to the site.

Browsing:
To scroll, use the scrollbar or trackpad.
Keep "Command" pressed.

CHAPTER EIGHT:
ALL ABOUT FACETIME CALLS

FaceTime Setup and Configuration

FaceTime, much like iMessage, is activated automatically using your phone number if you have an iPhone, but you have the option to use it using an email address instead of your phone number. This is similar to how iMessage works. However, if for some reason it is not working or if it has been switched off, you can follow the steps in the how to guide that is provided below. Getting FaceTime up and running is something that happens automatically after your iPhone is activated with a SIM card.

FaceTime must be activated.

- Launch the FaceTime app and enter your Apple ID and password to sign in. You also have the option to do this by going to Settings > FaceTime.
- When you use FaceTime on an iPhone, your phone number will be registered in the app automatically.

You have the ability to register your email address if you are using an iPhone or an iPad:

- Launch the Settings app.
- After selecting FaceTime, select. FaceTime requires that you sign in with your Apple ID.
- Please use your Apple ID to sign in.

Make a call using FaceTime.

- It is necessary to have the phone number or registered email address of the person you wish to call in order to use FaceTime. There are a number different ways that a FaceTime call can be made:
- Tap the "New FaceTime" button within the FaceTime app, and then type the contact's email address or phone number. After tapping the number or address, select Audio or FaceTime from the menu that appears.
- You can search for a person by starting to type their name and then tapping on their name when it shows in your Contacts3 list if you have the individual's phone number or email address saved for them. After that, select either the Audio or FaceTime icon.
- During a regular phone call, your iPhone also gives you the option to initiate a FaceTime video call. To switch to FaceTime, you can access it from the Phone app by tapping the FaceTime icon.
- Take a call from call waiting while you're on a FaceTime audio call.

You have the option of selecting one of the following alternatives whenever another call comes in, regardless of whether it is a phone call or another FaceTime audio call:

- The current call will be ended, and you will be prompted to accept the incoming call.
- The incoming call can be accepted, and the one you're now on will be put on hold while you take the new call.
- Refuse: You should refuse the incoming call.
- Transfer a call you're having on FaceTime to another device.
- It is required that all devices be running iOS 16, iPadOS 16, or later, as well as macOS Ventura.

You are able to transfer FaceTime calls from your iPhone to your Mac or iPad without any disruptions, and vice versa. When you transfer a call to another party, the connection of your Bluetooth headset automatically shifts to the new device at the same time.

HOW TO SNAP A PICTURE WHILE YOU'RE ON A FACETIME CALL

You should be able to capture a picture while you are on a FaceTime call as soon as you have FaceTime Live Photos enabled on your device. Having said that, there are a few important qualifications to make. The first need is that the other individuals on the FaceTime call also need to have FaceTime Live Photos activated on their device in order for you to be able to see them. The second limitation of using FaceTime Live Photos is that you cannot (luckily) utilize this capability to take a picture of someone else without that person being aware that you are doing so. Once the image has been taken, the app will send a notification to them.

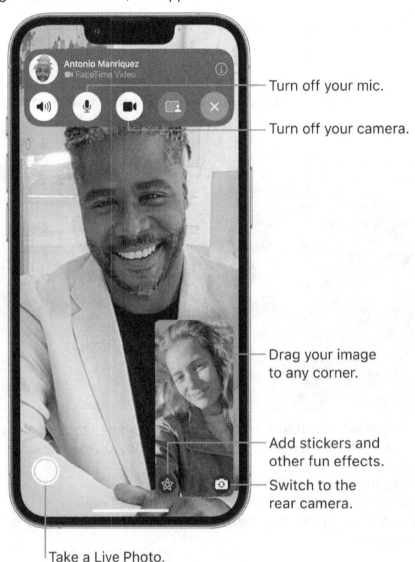

Turn off your mic.

Turn off your camera.

Drag your image to any corner.

Add stickers and other fun effects.

Switch to the rear camera.

Take a Live Photo.

HOW TO ACTIVATE FOCUS

These are the actions that need to be taken in order to activate the Focus mode on an iPhone or iPad that is running iOS 15 or a later version:

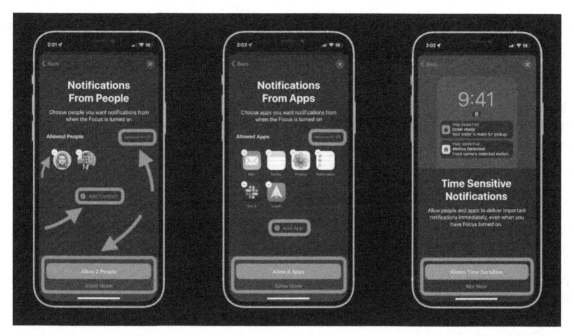

Switch on the Control Center:

On iPhones equipped with Face ID, swipe down from the top right corner of the screen. On older iPhone models or iPads equipped with a Home button, swipe up from the bottom edge of the screen.

Locate the Focus Mode:

Locate the icon that looks like a focus point in the Control Center. It resembles a crescent moon that is enclosed within a circle. Make sure you touch it.

Pick one of the Focus Modes:

You will be presented with a variety of Focus modes, such as Do Not Disturb, Personal, Work, and Sleep, amongst others. Simply select the option that you want to use by tapping on it.

Modify the Focus Mode as You See Fit :

Once you have chosen a Focus mode, you will have the opportunity to personalize it by tapping "Customize" or "Options." In this section, you will be given the opportunity to pick individual persons as well as apps that will be permitted to contact you while you are in Focus mode. You also have the option of setting up messages to receive automatic replies.

To use the Focus Mode, turn on:

After you have finished setting your Focus mode, you can turn it on by tapping the "Turn On" button. Your iPhone or iPad will now be operating in the Focus mode once you've made your selection.

Automate Focus Determination in Accordance with the Context:

Additionally, iOS 15 enables you to automate Focus modes according on your location, the time of day, or the patterns of your app usage. To set up automation, navigate to Settings > Focus > Focus Status and select "Automatically."

ENHANCING WELLNESS WITH YOUR IPHONE: A GUIDE TO NEW HEALTH FEATURES

The Health app's standout new feature is mood tracking, designed to assist you in monitoring your emotional state throughout the day and over time, pinpoint factors that influence your emotions, and evaluate how activities like physical exercise affect your mood.

How to monitor your mood with the health app

You have the option to log your mood multiple times a day and submit a daily overall mood via your Apple Watch or Health app notifications.

When you log a mood, you're presented with a slider ranging from Very Unpleasant to Neutral to Very Pleasant. You're tasked with moving the slider to the position that best reflects your current emotional state. The choices are color-coded (with very unpleasant as purple, neutral as blue, and very pleasant as orange).

Next, Apple presents you with a selection of mood-related terms, asking you to pick the one that most accurately describes your feeling. Options under "Very Pleasant" include Amazed, Peaceful, Joyful, and Calm, while "Very Unpleasant" includes emotions like Anger, Sadness, Fatigue, and Stress. Neutral options include feelings like Peaceful, Indifferent, and Content. You must choose from Apple's list and cannot add your own descriptor. The objective is simply to pick the closest match from the available options.

Apple then asks you to select a mood and a descriptive term before asking for the reason behind the mood. Choices include health, fitness, family, friends, relationships, dating, weather, finances, and current events, but you're restricted to Apple's list. However, you can add context in this part, providing more specifics about why you chose a certain category.

- To set up your initial mood or emotional state journal with iOS 17, follow these steps.
- Select the Browse tab in the Health app, then click on Mental Well-being under "Health Categories."
- Tap on State of Mind under "No Data Available."
- Click on Get Started.

- Choose to log your current feeling or your general mood for the day, then click Next.
- After using the slider to indicate your mood on a scale from Very Unpleasant to Very Pleasant, click Next.
- Pick the term that best describes this feeling, then click Next.
- After choosing the factor that most influences your mood from the list, click Done.
- You can view all your entries at any time using the State of Mind card in the Mental Well-being section of the Health app.

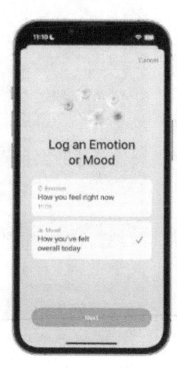
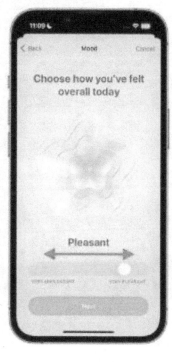

Setting Reminders to Log Your State of Mind

You can enable options in the Options menu at the bottom of the State of Mind section to remind you to log your mood during the day or at day's end.

If you prefer a more personalized reminder, you can set a specific time for it each day using the Choose Reminder... option. This is useful if you know when you're likely to experience certain mood triggers during your day.

How to set follow-up and critical medication reminders

Apple has enhanced the functionality in iOS 17 with the introduction of Follow-Up Reminders for any medications you monitor in the Health app. If you don't log a medication within 30 minutes of a standard reminder, you can opt to receive a second reminder to ensure you don't forget your intake. You can also enable Critical Alerts in addition to Follow-Up Reminders, which will appear on your iPhone's screen and sound an alarm even if Focus mode is active or the device is on silent.

Here's how to enable Follow-Up Medications in iOS 17 if you use the Health app to track your medication intake.

- In the Health app, select the Browse tab and then tap on Medications.
- Scroll to the bottom of the section and choose it.

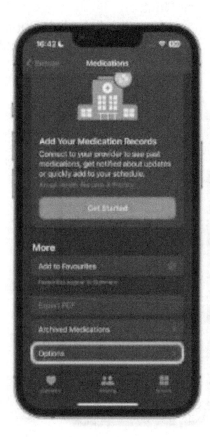 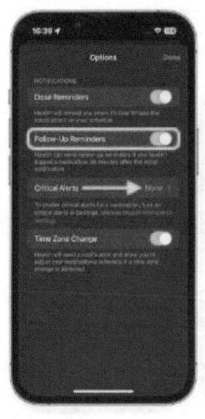 

- Turn on the Follow-Up Reminders option.
- If you want to enable them for one or all of your medications, tap on Critical Alerts.
- Turn on the toggles next to the medications for which you want to receive critical alerts. Confirm by tapping Allow when prompted.

How To Safeguard Your Eyes With The Screen Distance Tool

Of course, it's never too late to care for your eyes, which is why adults can also use the new Screen Distance feature. Screen Distance helps you maintain an optimal distance from your iPhone to reduce eye strain and the risk of myopia, especially in children. Apple provides a posture guide to help you understand the best position to hold the device for an optimal viewing experience without straining your eyes, recommending a viewing distance of 12 inches for the eyes.

Here's how to enable this new feature.

- Open the Settings app on your iPhone or iPad.
- Select Screen Time.
- Choose "Limit Usage," then "Screen Distance."
-

- Read the information screen before proceeding.
- Ensure the Screen Distance toggle is switched on by sliding it to the green position.

Apple's "Shield" will now notify you (or your child) if the iPhone or iPad is too close, suggesting you move it further away. Once the device is at the recommended distance, the shield will display a Continue button, allowing you to resume where you left off.

HOW TO GET WALKING DIRECTIONS WITH AUGUMENTED REALITY IN MAPS

What does "augmented reality" (AR) mean in the context of Google Maps?

You're about to find that using Google Maps is a lot less of a hassle for you. The upcoming updates to Google Maps' walking directions will be significant. You are about to obtain specific Augmented Reality maps and advice for Google Maps walking directions, and this is all thanks to machine learning, smart algorithms for positioning, and Google's Street View Technology. Since the introduction of Google Maps directions, this new experience, which Google refers to as "Global Localization," has quickly become one of the most popular and widely discussed developments. Let's get right down to it!

What is the functionality behind Google Maps AR?

Putting it succinctly, this technology provides a more powerful and intuitive method of assisting individuals in rapidly determining the direction they should move by using the camera on their smartphone as a sensor.

How to use augmented reality with Google Maps while walking?

How exactly does it function? The interface makes advantage of Google Street View to pinpoint the precise position of the user by'seeing' adjacent structures and landmarks that are already included in Street View's database. The user is then guided on the street by Augmented Reality (AR) technology, which projects directional arrows and other information onto the view captured by the camera on their smartphone. When compared to previous versions of Google Maps, this new update represents a significant advancement because it eliminates the need to look at the blue dot and then make educated guesses about where you are and in what direction you are facing.

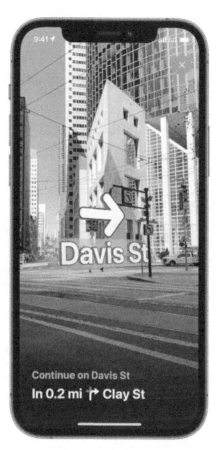

It is no longer necessary to follow that blue dot while peering into your screen in the hope that you won't run into anything. You will always have a clear view of what is in front of you when you use the AR camera. Once the precise location and direction have been determined, Google will also give you a prompt to put the phone down and stop moving about.

HOW TO USE SIRI TO SHARE WHAT'S ON YOUR SCREEN?

Set up a Shortcut for Siri Using the Following:

Open the Shortcuts application that's installed on your iOS device. This app is often already loaded on iOS devices, such as iPhones and iPads, when they are first purchased. You can create a new shortcut by hitting the "+" button that is found in the upper right corner of the screen. This will allow you to do so.

Click the "Add Action" button when you want to add some actions to your shortcut.

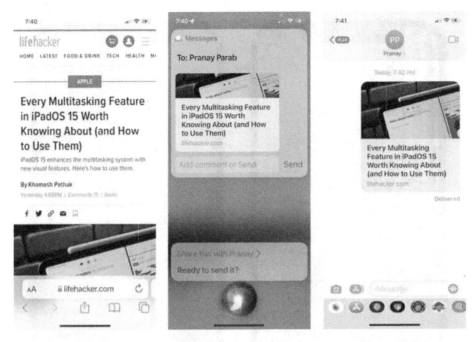

Take a screenshot and include it in your post action:

You have the ability to add an action to your shortcut by browsing the menu of possible actions for "Take Screenshot" and adding it. The operation you are about to do will record everything that is now displayed on your screen.

Include a Share Action by Declaring Something Like This:

After you have done adding the screenshot action, repeat the process of adding the action by tapping "Add Action" a second time, and then look for "Share" in the list of available actions.

Choose "Share" from the available options on the menu. As a result of this, it will now be possible for you to share the screenshot that you have just took.

Change your settings so that you can share:

Make the necessary adjustments in the event that you intend to share the snapshot with others. You can choose to send it via Messages, Mail, or any other app that is compatible with it. There are many options available to you.

What Should We Call It? Shortcuts

Tap the ellipsis (also known as three dots) that is placed in the top right corner of the screen in order to rename your shortcut. Because Siri will refer to the shortcut by the name you give it, it is vital to select a moniker that is simple and easy to recall.

Add the following to Siri:

To have Siri assist you in developing a distinctive voice command for your shortcut, all you have to do is tap the "Add to Siri" button. You may say something along the lines of "Share my screen" or you could use any other phrase that you choose. Simply following the on-screen steps will allow you to record your phrase. When you use this line going forward, Siri will realize that you are giving her an order to complete your shortcut, and she will do what you ask.

HOW TO USE APPLE MAPS TO LOCATE TRANSIT STATIONS NEAR YOU

Using Apple Maps to Obtain Directions Via Public Transportation From Point A to Point B

To get started, you will need to decide where you want to go. Either conduct a search for the location you want to visit, or select it from the list of your favorites.

Tap the car icon that appears next to see how much driving time is predicted to be required to reach the destination.

You will see icons that allow you to change the kind of directions you want to follow. These possibilities may include walking, taking public transportation, riding a bicycle, or participating in a ridesharing program, depending on what is available in your area.

Tap the icon that looks like the front of a bus to obtain directions using public transportation.

You have the ability to modify the time that you wish to leave or arrive, and immediately below that will be the route that takes the least amount of time.

If you swipe up, you will be presented with any more possibilities for transit routes that may be located in the immediate vicinity. Apple Maps not only shows you the bus routes you'll take, but it also estimates how long it will take you to walk to each station and between stops.

HOW TO USE SOS FUNCTION

Phone 15 Emergency SOS via Satellite:

What is it?

The Emergency SOS via satellite function allows your iPhone 15 to text emergency services when you're in places without cellular or Wi-Fi coverage. Think of it as a lifeline when you're in remote areas.

How to Prepare:

1. Medical ID: Before heading to areas without coverage, set up your Medical ID. This ID contains important health information that can be crucial in emergencies.

2. Emergency Contacts: Add contacts who should be notified in emergencies.

3. Demo Mode: Familiarize yourself with the feature by trying the Emergency SOS demo. Go to `Settings > Emergency SOS` and tap `Try Demo`.

How to Use:

1. If you're in an emergency and lack cellular or Wi-Fi or your local emergency number first.

2. If the call doesn't connect, tap `Emergency Text via Satellite`. Alternatively, open the Messages app or SOS, and select `Emergency Services`.

3. Tap `Report Emergency` and follow the on-screen instructions.

Tips for Best Use:

Ensure your phone has a clear view of the sky for the best satellite connection. You don't need to raise your phone high, but avoid heavy foliage or obstructions.

Once connected, your iPhone will share vital information like your Medical ID, emergency contact details, your location, and battery level with the emergency services. If you've set them up, your emergency contacts will also receive this information.

You can also proactively share your location using the Find My app when you're without cellular or Wi-Fi coverage.

Remember, this feature is designed to help you in emergencies, especially when you're in areas without regular phone coverage. It's always a good idea to familiarize yourself with it and set up the necessary details before you might need it.

USE YOUR IPHONE OR IPAD TO LAUNCH FACETIME

While use an iPhone:

Through the use of Siri:

Siri can be activated on your device by saying "Hey Siri," pushing and holding the Side button (on iPhone models with Face ID), or pressing and holding the Home button (on iPhone models with a Home button). Saying "Hey Siri" also works.

Just say the word "FaceTime" to Siri, and she will open the FaceTime app for you automatically.

Using the Spotlight Search Function to Find Something:

You may access the Spotlight Search by swiping down from the centre of the Home screen when you are on that screen.

If you type "FaceTime" into the search area, the icon for the FaceTime app should appear in the list of results that the search generates for you. The application can be started by just tapping on the button.

Using the Application's Icon to Your Advantage:

Going to the Home screen of your iPhone will allow you to locate the symbol for the FaceTime app. It's an emblem that appears like a camera on the outside, but inside it's a video camera that's white.

To start using the FaceTime app, you have to press on the program's icon. This is the only requirement to use the software.

When use an iPad:

Through the use of Siri:

Siri can be activated on your device by saying "Hey Siri" or by touching the Home button (on iPad models from the past) or the Side button (on iPad Pro models that do not have a Home button).

Just say the word "FaceTime" to Siri, and she will open the FaceTime app for you automatically.

Using the Spotlight Search Function to Find Something:

You may access the Spotlight Search by swiping down from the centre of the Home screen when you are on that screen.

If you type "FaceTime" into the search area, the icon for the FaceTime app should appear in the list of results that the search generates for you. The application can be started by just tapping on the button.

Utilization of the Dock in the Following:

If you already have FaceTime in your Dock (the bar that runs along the bottom of the screen), all you have to do to activate the application is press on the icon that represents it. If you don't currently have FaceTime in your Dock, you can download it from the Apple website. In the event that it is not already present in the Dock, you have the option of adding it there so that it is easier to reach.

UNLOCK WITH AN APPLE WATCH NOT WORKING? HERE IS HOW TO SOLVE THE PROBLEM

If you try to unlock your iPhone with your Apple Watch and it does not work as you would anticipate, there are a few troubleshooting steps you can go through to fix the problem. This is how you should go about diagnosing and fixing the issue:

1. Make Certain That Both of Your Devices Are Compatible:

Check that your iPhone and Apple Watch are both capable of using the Unlock with Apple Watch feature by following the instructions above. This feature necessitates the use of an iPhone equipped with Face ID as well as an Apple Watch running watchOS 7 or a later version.

2. Verify That Your Bluetooth and Wi-Fi Connections Are Working

Check to see that the Bluetooth and Wi-Fi settings on both your iPhone and Apple Watch are turned on. In order for the feature to function, both of the devices need to be linked to the same Wi-Fi network and within Bluetooth range (which is typically about 30 feet or 10 meters).

3. Check the Following Settings on Your Apple Watch:

Go to Settings on your Apple Watch, then select Passcode, and then select Wrist Detection. Check to see that the Wrist Detection feature is active. This function verifies that your Apple Watch is already unlocked and that it is attached to your wrist before allowing it to unlock your iPhone.

Verify further that the "Unlock with iPhone" feature is turned on. Navigate to the Settings menu on your Apple Watch, then select the Passcode option. Then, select Unlock with iPhone. If it isn't already, you should turn it on now.

4. Check the Settings on Your iPhone:

To enable Face ID and a passcode on your iPhone, navigate to Settings > Face ID & Passcode. When prompted, enter the passcode that you have been given.

Make sure the option to "Unlock with Apple Watch" is activated in the settings.

5. Make Sure You Have the Latest Software Updates:

Check to see that the most recent software updates have been installed on both your iPhone and your Apple Watch. Updates to the software can frequently fix any problems that may have been occurring.

6. Ensure That Both Devices Are Restarted:

You should restart your iPhone as well as your Apple Watch. This little procedure can frequently resolve a wide variety of connectivity problems.

7. To delete your Face ID:

In the event that nothing else works, you can attempt to reset the Face ID on your iPhone. Navigate to the Settings menu, then select Face ID & Passcode, and then select Reset Face ID. Reconfigure it and check to see whether the problem still exists after you've done so.

8. Re-pair Your Apple Watch: Resetting Your Watch

You can always try to unpair your Apple Watch and then re-pair it if all else fails. Because doing this will cause all of the settings on your Apple Watch to be reset, you should make sure that you have a backup of your data before continuing.

CHAPTER NINE:
SIRI

Apple Inc.'s iOS, iPadOS, watchOS, and macOS operating systems all support the virtual assistant known as Siri, which was developed by Apple Inc. Voice recognition and natural language processing are both put to use in order to decipher and reply to orders and questions posed by users. Siri is capable of performing a wide variety of operations, including but not limited to the following: scheduling reminders, sending and receiving text messages and phone calls, delivering weather updates, offering answers to general knowledge queries, and managing smart home devices.

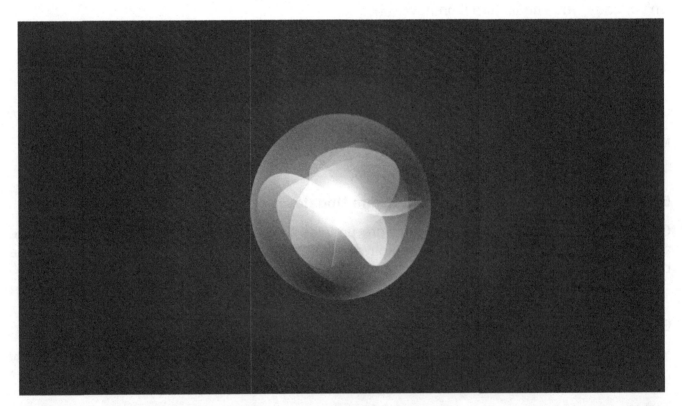

Users can activate Siri on compatible Apple devices by issuing the voice command "Hey Siri" or by pushing a button that is specifically dedicated for this purpose. Apple consumers now have a hands-free and more comfortable method to engage with their Apple devices thanks to Siri, which is designed to learn from user interactions and personalize responses over time. Siri is designed to learn from user interactions.

HOW TO TELL SIRI TO CONTROL YOUR HOME KIT DEVICES AT A PREDETERMINED TIME

Install and Configure Your HomeKit Devices

You will need to add your HomeKit-compatible smart devices as accessories in the Home app before you can begin using Siri to control them. HomeKit-compatible smart devices can be found here. This is because Siri recognizes your accessories based on the names you've given them, as well as their locations and any other information you've given them through the Home app.

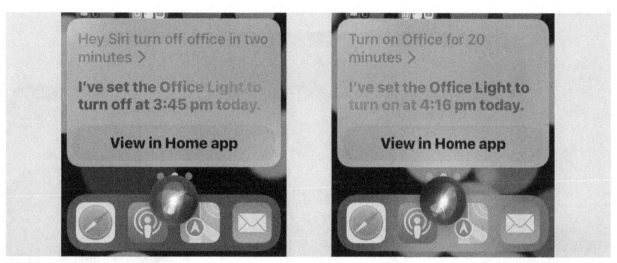

Create a Home Networking Hub

In addition, if you wish to control your accessories when you are away from home, you will need to set up a home hub. To do so, click on one of the links below to configure the device to function as a home hub.

You may use HomePod as a HomeKit Home Hub by configuring it.

HomeKit may be used to turn Apple TV into a home hub.

HomeKit Home Hub functionality can be enabled on iPad.

Siri Commands for the HomeKit System

Continue reading if you want to learn some common instances of Siri commands that you may use to control your HomeKit devices once you have finished setting up your home accessories in the Home app.

Turn on or off the Accessories as needed.

"Turn on the lights," the voice said.

"Turn off the ventilation fan."

"Flip the switch to turn the light on."

"Hey Siri, create an atmosphere for reading."

"Turn on the stove or the heater."

Modify one of the Accessories.

"Adjust the thermostat so that it reads 65 degrees."

"Lower the brightness in the second floor to sixty percent."

"Turn the lights in the bedroom all the way up."

"The lights in the living room should be changed to a purple hue."

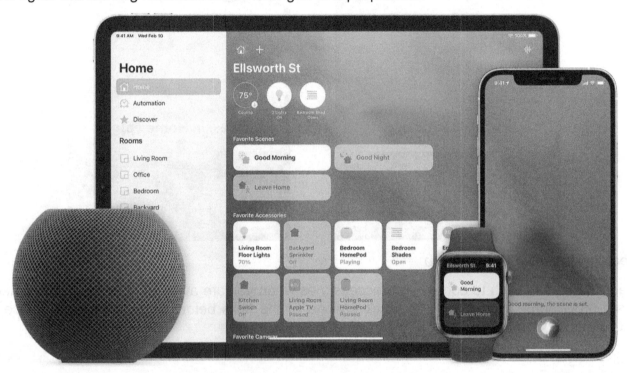

Take Command of a Space or Area

"Turn off the lights in the upstairs."

"Start the fan in the storage room," the voice said.

"Begin to heat the downstairs immediately."

Prepare the Stage

"Hey Siri, I hope you have a good night."

"Hey, Siri! I've arrived at home."

HOW TO MAKE SIRI READ YOUR NOTIFICATION

The following is a guide on how to make Siri announce notifications in iOS 15.

- Launch the app that controls settings.
- Choose the Notifications option
- Select the "Announce Notifications" option available through the "Siri" menu.
- Move the switch that is adjacent to Announce Notifications so that it is in the green ON position.
- Simply select the app from the drop-down menu labeled "Announce" to have Siri provide all of the notifications from a single program.
- Notifications From" and make sure the option to Announce Notifications is checked.

HOW TO USE THE AUTOMATIC TRANSLATION OF THE TRANSLATE APPLICATION?

To start utilizing automatic translation, you must first enter conversation mode by pressing on the Conversation tab, which can be found at the bottom of the screen regardless of whether the device is oriented in portrait or landscape mode. Once you have done this, you may begin using automatic translation. Any direction is acceptable when carrying out these steps.

To access the ellipsis, located in the bottom-right corner, tap the icon that looks like three dots.

Make your selection using the drop-down option labeled Automatic Translation when it appears.

The Translate software can now detect when you begin and end speaking, enabling the other person to respond without having to engage with the iPhone directly

HOW TO QUICKLY REFRESH A WEB PAGE IN SAFARI

You can still reload the website that you are currently seeing by pressing the refresh icon that is located in the URL bar of Apple products. On the other hand, there is now an additional option for refreshing web sites that is less obvious and that you might find more convenient.

When using Safari, all that is required to refresh a webpage is a downward swipe on the page in question. This alternative to tapping the reload icon is especially helpful if you like to keep the address bar at the top of the screen, in which case tapping the icon to reload the page could be problematic.

HOW TO CHANGE THE HOME PAGE AND BACKGROUND OF SAFARI?

When using an iPhone or an iPad, launch Safari.

Tap the open tabs icon that is located in the bottom right corner of the screen while using Safari.

Simply press the "Plus" sign that can be found in the bottom left corner of the Tabs display to open a new tab. To edit the Start Page, scroll down to the bottom of the page and click the Edit button.

You can synchronize the settings of your Start Page with additional devices linked to the same Apple ID by activating the button that is located next to the phrase "Use Start Page on All Devices."

Utilizing the switches, you may manage the content that is displayed on your Start Page. The home page of Safari includes the following sections: Favorites, Frequently Visited, Shared with You, Privacy Report, Siri Suggestions, Reading List, and iCloud Tabs. Any of these sections can be seen by the user.

You may also enable the Background image option by selecting the huge Plus icon. From there, you can select one of the wallpapers that come pre-installed on iOS devices or make your own using your own pictures. When you are finished, you can close the menu card by tapping the X in the upper-right corner of the screen.

HOW TO USE TAB GROUPS IN SAFARI?

Launch Safari by touching the icon that looks like two open books in the lower right-hand corner of the screen.

Tap the tab bar at the bottom of the screen in the middle, then either press and hold it or tap it.

Pick the option to create a new empty tab group. You also have the option of selecting New Tab Group from X Tabs if you already have the tabs that you desire to merge open in the browser.

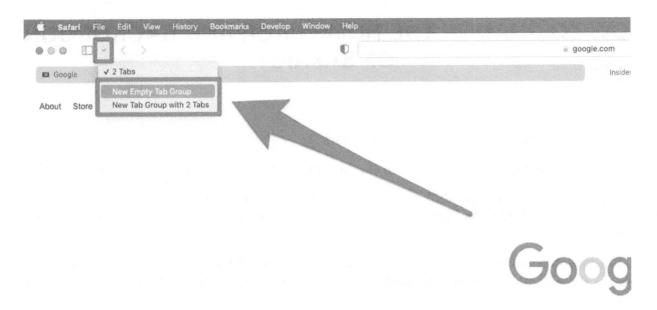

After giving your Tab Group a name, click the Save button to commit the changes.

When you have created one or more Tab Groups, you can rapidly navigate between them by hitting the Tab bar in the open tabs view and selecting the desired group from the drop-down menu that appears. When a Tab Group is chosen, any new tabs that are launched will automatically be added to the selected group.

INQUIRE OF SIRI

Getting things done quickly and easily can be accomplished through conversation with Siri. You may ask Siri to translate a word, set an alarm, identify a location, provide information on the weather, and much more.

Siri may be activated by the sound of your voice.

Hey Siri, who are you?

Product Case Study of Apple's Voice Assistant

When activated using your voice, Siri will speak its responses to you aloud.

Say "Hey Siri," then ask Siri a question or give her a task once you have finished saying "Hey Siri."

If you want to ask Siri another question or have her perform another action, you can either repeat "Hey Siri" or tap the Listen button.

Note: If you want to stop your iPhone from answering when you say "Hey Siri," just turn it upside down.

Pressing a Button Will Activate Siri

Siri is activated by pressing a button on the iPhone; however, while the iPhone is set to silent mode, Siri's responses are muted. When the silent mode is turned off, Siri will respond with an audible response. To make changes to this, go to the page where you can adjust Siri's response.

Maintain pressure on the button on the side.

When Siri appears, you will have the opportunity to pose a question to her or request that she perform an action on your behalf.

Simply ask Siri another question by tapping the Listen button, or on to the next activity.

If Siri has misunderstood you, feel free to correct her.

In response to the question you posed: After you have reworded your inquiry, you can play the Listen button.

Make the following adjustments to a message before you send it: Make the proclamation, "Change it."

If you see the words on the screen, you have the ability to make changes to your request using that text. Tap the request using the virtual keyboard that appears on the screen.

Add Shortcuts for Siri Certain programs feature shortcuts for tasks that you perform regularly, and you can add these shortcuts to Siri. You need just use your voice to activate Siri in order to use any of these shortcuts.

CHARGE IPHONE WITH MAGSAFE CHARGER

Connect the MagSafe Charger to the power supply using the Apple USB-C 20W power adapter or any other power adapter that supports the USB-C standard.

The USB cable should be used to connect the charger to the iPhone, its MagSafe case, or its sleeve, respectively. You will notice an icon on your screen that indicates that your iPhone is charging as soon as it begins to charge.

Establish a connection between your iPhone and Apple Watch.

Tap the Apple Watch app on your iPhone, and then proceed with the instructions that appear on the screen.

Using your Apple Watch, you can unlock your iPhone.

You may use your Apple Watch to unlock your iPhone in a secure manner provided that you also use a face mask.

Take the following steps in order to enable Apple Watch to unlock your iPhone:

Navigate to Settings > Face ID and Passcode on your device's menu.

Followed by activating Apple Watch, which can be found below the "Unlock with Apple Watch" option.

If you have more than one watch, you need to make sure the setting is active on each one.

While you are wearing an Apple Watch and a face mask, you can wake up your iPhone by raising or pressing the screen, and then you can unlock it by looking at it.

Your Apple Watch must be equipped with a passcode, unlocked, and worn on your wrist in addition to being in close proximity to your iPhone in order for you to be able to unlock your iPhone with it.

THINGS SIRI CAN DO ON IPHONE

You can access information and do activities by utilizing Siri on your iPhone. Siri and its response will appear on top of what you are currently doing, enabling you to refer to information that is displayed on the screen.

A chatbot is what Siri is. You have the option of tapping a web link that Siri provides in order to access it in your default web browser and discover additional information about it. If the on-screen response provided by Siri contains buttons or other controls, you can tap those to do additional actions. You also have the option of asking Siri another question or having her carry out an additional task for you.

The following is a list of some instances of what you can ask Siri to do. Additional examples can be found at various points throughout this session. You also have the option of asking Siri the following queries: "Hey Siri, what can you do?" is one of the inquiries you may ask.

You can get the answers to your questions by using Siri.

It is possible to utilize Siri to check facts, conduct computations, or translate a statement into another language in a very short amount of time.

Utilize Siri in conjunction with Applications.

Siri gives you the ability to use your voice to control apps. Say something along the lines of "Hey Siri, create an event in the Calendar for a meeting with Gordon at 9 a.m." and see what happens.

Say something like "Hey Siri, add artichokes to my grocery list," and the item will be added to your list of reminders.

"Hey, Siri, what's the latest update on my status?" to maintain an up-to-date status on local weather, current happenings, reminders, and calendar events, among other things.

For additional illustrations, take a look at any one of the following:

It is possible to utilize the iPhone's Siri feature to announce incoming calls, texts, and other events. You can use Siri to play music on your iPhone, and you can use Apple Music Voice to listen to music on your iPhone. You are able to exercise control over your home by using Siri on your iPhone.

Use Siri, Maps, or the Maps widget on your iPhone to locate the directions you need.

Turn on the iPhone's Siri Shortcuts feature.

You Can Communicate with Your Contacts Using Siri to Share Information.

You are able to share onscreen objects with anyone in your contacts, such as photographs, websites, content from Apple Music or Apple Podcasts, places on Maps, and more.

Saying something of the effect of "Hey Siri, send this to mum" when you are looking at a photo in your Photo library, for instance, will cause a new message to be generated that contains the photo.

How to Enable Commands Beginning with "Hey Siri" on an iPhone 15 Pro Max

The voice command "Hey Siri" is the technique to interact with Siri in the most natural way possible. If you didn't turn on this feature when you were setting up your iPhone for the first time, you should go ahead and do it now.

Launch the "Settings" application that's on your iPhone 15 Pro Max.

Choose "Siri and Search" from the list of options in the drop-down menu. Select it to open up this collection of available options.

You can hear "Hey Siri" simply toggling the switch on the right side of the device.

In order to register your voice, you will need to follow the instructions that show on your screen.

You are now free to close the Settings app and begin utilizing Siri after you have completed the previous steps.

CHAPTER TEN:
HANDOVER WORK THROUGH YOUR IPHONE AND OTHER DEVICES

You are able to begin something on one device, such as your iPhone, iPad, iPod touch, or Mac, and finish it on another device, such as your iPhone, iPad, iPod touch, or Mac, or even your Apple Watch. This is made possible by the Handoff feature.

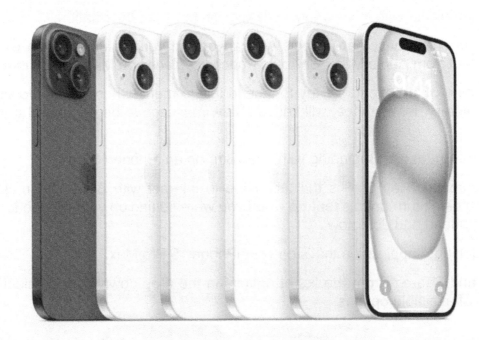

You can, for instance, begin composing a response to an email on your iPhone and then finish it in Mail on your Mac. Handoff is compatible with a wide range of applications developed by Apple, such as Calendar, Contacts, and Safari.

There is a possibility that certain applications developed by third parties are also compatible with Handoff.

Before getting started

Ensure the following on both your iPhone and any other devices you use, and tasks will be able to be moved across them:

Both of these gadgets are linked to the same Apple ID on Apple's servers.

Wi-Fi allows your electronic devices to establish a connection to the internet.

Your Bluetooth-enabled devices can communicate with one another up to a distance of approximately 33 feet (10 meters).

On your Mac, Handoff can be activated in the System Preferences menu under General, and Bluetooth can be activated in the System Preferences menu under Bluetooth.

Your iPhone and any other iOS or iPadOS device both have Handoff enabled in Settings > General > AirPlay and Handoff, and Bluetooth is turned on in Settings.

Every piece of hardware is operating with the most recent update of the essential software: T is for the following: iOS 10, iPadOS 13, macOS 10.10, or watchOS 1.0.

TRANSFER FROM A DIFFERENT DEVICE TO YOUR IPHONE

Launch the App Switcher on your iPhone right now. The Handoff icon for the application that you are currently using on your other device appears at the bottom of the screen on your iPhone.

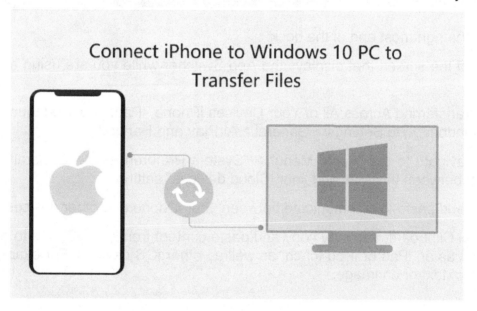

Connect iPhone to Windows 10 PC to Transfer Files

Tap the symbol that looks like a hand to carry on working in the app.

TRANSFER FROM IPHONE TO ANOTHER DEVICE

Simply tap or click the Handoff icon on the screen of the other device to go on working in the app there.

The Handoff icon for the app that you are currently using on your iPhone appears in the following places on other devices, including but not limited to:

Mac: The right-hand side of the Dock (or the bottom of the Dock, depending on where you have the Dock positioned).

The iPad is at the rightmost end of the dock.

At the bottom of the screen that displays the App Switcher while you are using an iPhone or an iPod touch.

Incapable of Transferring Across All of Your Devices iPhone, iPad, and iPod touch: To configure AirPlay and Handoff, go to Settings > General > AirPlay and Handoff.

On the Mac, navigate to the "Apple Menu" > "System Preferences" > "General" to turn off the "Allow Handoff between this Mac and your iCloud devices" setting.

Use cut, copy, and paste to communicate between your iPhone and other devices.

Using Universal Clipboard, you may copy and paste content from your iPhone to a Mac, another iOS device, like as an iPad or iPod touch, as well as other iOS devices. For example, you could copy a section of text or an image.

Ahead of the Beginning

Take the following safety procedures whenever you are transferring content from your iPhone to another device by cutting, copying, or pasting:

Both of these gadgets are linked to the same Apple ID on Apple's servers.

Your gadgets can connect to the internet via Wi-Fi.

Bluetooth connectivity is available between your devices at a distance of approximately 33 feet or 10 meters.

On the iPhone and any other iOS or iPadOS device, you can turn on Handoff by going to Settings > General > AirPlay and Handoff. Additionally, you can turn on Bluetooth by going to Settings.

You can activate Handoff on a Mac by going to System Preferences > General, and you can activate Bluetooth by going to System Preferences > Bluetooth.

Every gadget is operating with the most recent version of iOS, iPadOS, or macOS—iOS 10, iPadOS 13, or macOS 10.12, respectively. The three C's: copy, cut, and paste.

Make a mark on the paper by pressing three fingers together.

To close the cut, pinch the tips of three consecutive fingers together twice.

Pinch the paste open with all three of your fingers. In addition, you can choose an item by touching and holding it, and then selecting either Cut, Copy, or Paste from the menu that appears.

Important: Please keep in mind that the time allotted for you to cut, copy, and paste your text is very limited.

HOW TO CONNECT TO A BLUETOOTH DEVICE

On your iPhone, navigate to the Settings > Bluetooth menu. To make use of the function, you must push the button that is located next to the word "Bluetooth."

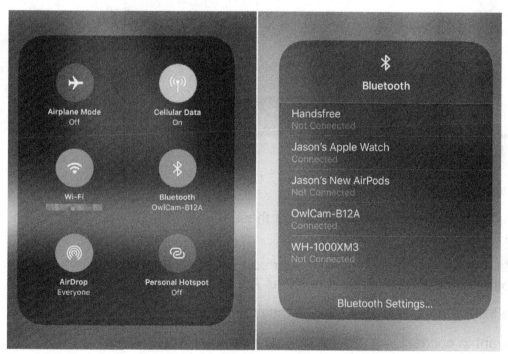

To connect your phone to the Bluetooth device, you will need to press the required Bluetooth device and then follow the on-screen instructions on the computer monitor.

To access the home screen, drag your finger up from the bottom of the screen in the direction of the arrow.

SYNC YOUR IPHONE WITH YOUR PC

You may use iCloud to automatically synchronize your images, files, calendars, and any other data that is stored on any device that is enabled with your Apple ID. (You can even view your iCloud data on iCloud.com using a computer running the Windows operating system.) With third-party services like as Apple Music, you may access more material across all of your devices simultaneously.

In the event that you do not choose to make use of iCloud or any other services, the following things might be synchronized with your iPhone:

Albums, singles, playlists, films, television programs, podcasts, audiobooks, novels, pictures, and video snippets are all examples of media that can be found in this category.

To-do lists and appointment books

You may maintain the most recent version of these items on both your iPhone and computer by syncing the two devices.

It is possible that the option to sync with your computer will not be available if you use iCloud or any of the other cloud-based services, such as Apple Music.

Put in place Your iPhone and your Mac so they can sync.

When you want to connect your iPhone to your computer, you will need a cable.

Choose your iPhone from the options presented to you in the Finder sidebar on your Mac.

At the very top of the window, you will see a drop-down menu where you may select the category of material you desire to synchronize.

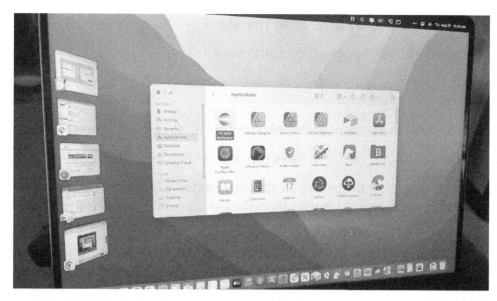

From the drop-down box, select the option to Sync [kind of content] to [name of device].

You have the option to sync only specific things, such as music, movies, books, or calendars, as opposed to the full content category if you so want.

Repeat steps 3 and 4 from the previous section for each category of content you desire to synchronize, and then click the Apply button.

HOW TO SEND CONTENT FROM AN IPHONE TO A COMPUTER?

iCloud Drive gives you the ability to keep all of your devices, including Windows PCs, synced with the most recent versions of your data. You may use AirDrop to send email attachments, transfer files between iPhones and other devices, and transfer files between iPhones and other devices.

How can I transfer files from my iPhone to my Mac?

Establish a connection between your iPhone and your PC.

You can connect by using a USB cable, or you can use a Wi-Fi connection if the Wi-Fi sync feature is turned on.

Choose your iPhone from the options presented to you in the Finder sidebar on your Mac.

To access any of the following, click the Files tab at the very top of the Finder window.

You can move a file or group of folders from one Finder window to another by dragging and dropping them onto the name of an application that is currently being transferred from a Mac to an iPhone.

In order to transfer files from an iPhone to a Mac: You can move a file from the files list on your iPhone to a Finder window by clicking the disclosure triangle that is located next to the name of the application.

How to Transfer Files from Your iPhone to Your Computer.

You may get the latest version of iTunes for your PC by installing it or upgrading it.

Use the USB cord that came with your iPhone to connect it to a computer running Windows.

You can connect by using a USB cable, or you can connect over a Wi-Fi connection if the Wi-Fi syncing feature is activated.

On your Windows computer, open iTunes and look for the iPhone button in the window's upper left corner. After clicking File Sharing, select an application from the list, and then perform one of the following actions: The process of transferring a file from your iPhone to your computer may be broken down into the following steps: Select the file that you want to move from the list on the right, then click "Store too," navigate to the location where you want the file to be saved, and then click "Save To" at the bottom of the window.

The following steps need to be taken in order to transfer a file from your computer to your iPhone: Click the Add button, then navigate to the location of the file you wish to send.

Establish a connection between your iPhone and a computer. Utilizing the USB Cable for a Number of Different Purposes

iPhone configuration.

Fees will be assessed for the Internet connection on the iPhone. The place to be

Transfer of files

Either directly or by use of an adapter, connect the iPhone's USB cable to the computer's USB port, then connect the computer's USB port to the USB cable.

Passing the Baton

You are able to pick up on another device exactly where you left off on another device thanks to a function called "Handoff."

Task handoff works with a wide variety of Apple applications, including Mail, Safari, Pages, Numbers, Keynote, Maps, Messages, Reminders, and Calendar, amongst others.

It is required that the devices be within a range of approximately 10 meters and have Bluetooth switched on.

Continuity with Handoff:

Once you have logged into the MacBook Pro, iOS device, or iPadOS device with the same Apple ID and have enabled Wi-Fi and Bluetooth, an icon will appear in the Dock whenever an activity is being handed off. This feature is only available if Wi-Fi and Bluetooth are enabled. On your MacBook Pro, you can be reading content on a website, and then you can use Handoff to transfer that information to your iPhone and continue reading where you left off. Handoff is compatible with a wide variety of Apple applications; however, all of the participating devices' operating systems must be up to date. To activate Handoff, navigate to the System Preferences menu on your Mac, choose the General tab, and then select the Allow Handoff option.

Handoff can be disabled by navigating to System Preferences > General > Allow Handoff this Mac and your iCloud devices but deselecting the option to "Allow Handoff this Mac and your iCloud devices." This will disable "Handoff" on your Mac. Handoff can be disabled by going to Settings > General > Airplay and Handoff on any of your iOS devices (iPhone, iPad, or iPad Touch).

Take control of aircraft mode: If you are going to be traveling with your iPhone or are going to be in a location that does not allow wireless communication, you can keep the device turned on but in airplane mode. You can take notes, listen to music, watch movies, read books, play games, and engage in a variety of other activities while your device is set to airplane mode because these activities do not require internet connectivity. Navigate to the Control Center > Airplane Mode menu option, then click to activate Bluetooth or Wi-Fi. When you are ready to leave airplane mode, you can quit the mode by turning it off.

HOW TO ERASE IPHONE

It's possible that you'll need to erase your iPhone in order to completely remove all of your data, content, and settings from it, even after you've deleted them. To delete all content and settings, navigate to Settings > General > Reset > Enter Passcode > Erase All Content.

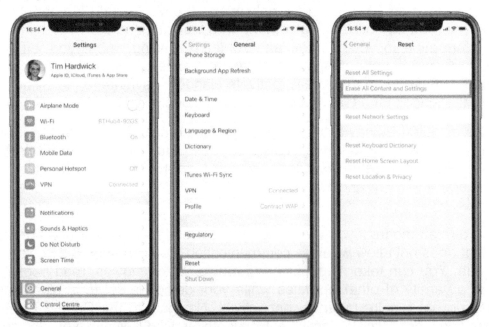

It is imperative that you create a backup and wipe your iPhone before handing it over to another person so that they can use it.

RESTORE IPHONE TO DEFAULT SETTINGS

It is possible to return your iPhone to its factory settings without necessarily wiping all of the content from your device. Navigate to the Settings menu, then select General, then Reset, and finally Reset All Settings. The network settings, keyboard dictionary, location settings, privacy settings, and Apply Pay settings would all be reset as a result of this action. The information and media that have been stored on the phone are not lost or removed in any way.

You can also reset individual settings on the iPhone; this does not clear all of the settings. Configuration options include things like the network settings, the keyboard dictionary, the home screen layout, as well as the location and privacy options.

Navigate to the Settings menu, then select General, and then Transfer or Reset iPhone.

You can also use the additional free storage space provided by iCloud in the event that you are deleting your iPhone in order to replace it with a new iPhone that you already own. This will allow you to move all of your programs and data to the new device. After selecting Get Started, navigate to the Settings menu, then select General, and finally, Transfer or Reset iPhone.

Next, pick "Erase All Content and Settings" from the available menu options.

When you restart your iPhone, all of the content and settings will be destroyed. At this point, you have the option of restoring it from a backup or configuring it as if it were brand new.

HOW TO USE PC TO RESET IPHONE 15?

It is possible to return your iPhone to its factory settings without necessarily wiping all of the content from your device. Navigate to the Settings menu, then select General, then Reset, and finally Reset All Settings. The network settings, keyboard dictionary, location settings, privacy settings, and Apply Pay settings would all be reset as a result of this action. The information and media that have been stored on the phone are not lost or removed in any way.

You can also reset individual settings on the iPhone; this does not clear all of the settings. Configuration options include things like the network settings, the keyboard dictionary, the home screen layout, as well as the location and privacy options.

Navigate to the Settings menu, then select General, and then Transfer or Reset iPhone. You can also use the additional free storage space provided by iCloud in the event that you are deleting your iPhone in order to replace it with a new iPhone that you already own. This will allow you to move all of your programs and data to the new device. After selecting Get Started, navigate to the Settings menu, then select General, and finally, Transfer or Reset iPhone.

Next, pick "Erase All Content and Settings" from the available menu options.

When you restart your iPhone, all of the content and settings will be destroyed. At this point, you have the option of restoring it from a backup or configuring it as if it were brand new.

IPHONE APPS AND FEATURES

There are a lot of great applications that come preloaded on the iPhone, and all of them will help you become more productive by making it possible for you to do a wider variety of tasks in a shorter amount of time.

The following applications and functions are either included with the iPhone as standard equipment or can be downloaded through the App Store.

You can use Airdrop to send and receive documents, photographs, map locations, files, and webpages wirelessly (through Wi-Fi and Bluetooth) to a nearby Mac, iPhone, or iPad. Airdrop also allows you to share locations on a map.

Send and receive files with Airdrop: Simply select the object you wish to send by clicking on it, then go to the Share menu, click on Airdrop, and then click on the user profile image of someone who is nearby. Click the Airdrop button within the Finder app, and then drag the file over to the device of the receiver. It is up to the recipient to decide whether or not they will accept the file before the sharing process can be finalized.

Receive files with the use of Airdrop: Make sure that the "Allow me to be discovered" option is selected in the AirDrop window, and then select the appropriate setting in Control Center (nobody, contacts, or everyone). To accept an Airdrop, navigate to the notification and then click the Accept button that appears. The downloaded file will, by default, be placed in the Downloads folder when it is received.

Because Airdrop uses Bluetooth, the Bluetooth feature of both devices needs to be turned on and they must be within 30 feet (9 meters) of each other in order for it to work

CHAPTER ELEVEN
HOW TO USE "HIDE MY EMAIL" TO CREATE AN EMAIL ADDRESS

iCloud+ gives you access to a feature called Hide My Email, which allows you to conceal your personal email address from other people. while you use Hide My Email, you may generate one-of-a-kind, random email addresses that will forward to your personal email account. This will allow you to avoid disclosing your actual email address while you are filling out online forms or signing up for online newsletters, as well as when you are sending emails.

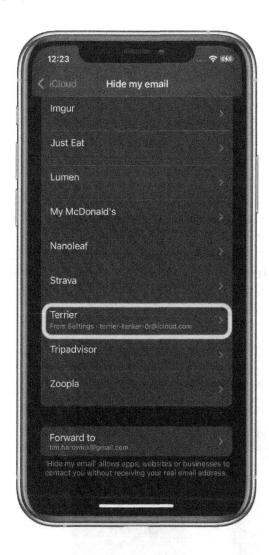

In the Settings menu, you'll find options to both create and manage your "Hide My Email" addresses. You can hide your email by following any of these steps after going to Settings > [your name] > iCloud > Hide My Email:

- Establish a Cover My electronic mail address is: Tap the button labeled Create New Address, then follow the directions that appear on the screen.

- Put a Hide into Inactive Mode My electronic mail address is: Tap an address, then tap the Deactivate Email Address button that appears underneath the Create New Address button. After you deactivate the address, you will no longer receive emails that are sent to that address.
- Modify the personal email address that the forwarding will be sent to: Tap the Forward To button, then select an email address from the drop-down menu. Your Apple ID gives you access to a list of addresses, which you can choose from as options.
- Make a copy of the forwarding address to use it in another context: Copy an address by first selecting it below the "Create New Address" option, then touching and holding the "Hide My Email" portion. Simply press and hold an empty text area, then tap the Paste button to immediately utilize the URL somewhere else.

HOW TO KEEP YOUR IP ADDRESS PRIVATE WHILE USING SAFARI?

What exactly is a person's IP address?

Internet Protocol is what "IP" stands for. Every device that is linked to the internet or a private network is assigned what is known as an IP address, which is a number or address that is completely unique to that device. It assists in the identification of electronic gadgets while using the internet. An Internet Protocol (IP) address is a string or series of digits that are separated by a decimal point, such as 192.135.2. There are four different varieties of Internet Protocol (IP) addresses: public, private, dynamic, and static. There is only one public IP address in existence, and it can be seen by everybody who uses the internet. A static IP address is one that cannot be modified or updated in any way. Your Internet Protocol address might be IPv4 or IPv6.

IP-based geolocation refers to the process of detecting the geographic position of an internet-connected electronic equipment based on that device's IP addresses. This information typically consists of geographical location data, which may include the country, state, region, city, latitude, and longitude coordinates. An advanced IP finder such as ipstack will also return information pertaining to the area code, time zone, and currency associated with the IP address that was requested.

How Can I Hide My IP Address on My Mac And iPhone?

On both the iPhone and the Mac, there are a number of different methods that you may safeguard your online privacy by hiding your IP address.

How Can I hide My Real IP Address When Connecting My iPhone to a VPN Service?

The abbreviation VPN refers to a Virtual Private Network. Your internet connection and your ability to maintain your online anonymity are both safeguarded by a virtual private network, or VPN. In most cases, virtual private networks (VPNs) are utilized to conceal IP addresses in order to get around geographical restrictions imposed by streaming video providers such as Netflix. On the other hand, you may also use it to conceal your IP address and safeguard your privacy while you're online.

A virtual private network, or VPN, works by essentially establishing a connection between your device and the internet that is both encrypted and safe. As a direct consequence of this, websites and applications are unable to view your true IP address. Instead, the IP address of the server is what is displayed to them. Overall, a virtual private network (VPN) will encrypt your data and give you a new IP address, which will mask the original one. For instance, a virtual private network (VPN) can be utilized to get an IP address from another nation.

There are many free virtual private network (VPN) services now available on the market. On the other hand, a premium version is typically more effective, and fortunately, paid VPNs may be found at relatively cheap price points. ExpressVPN, NordVPN, and PureVPN are some of the greatest virtual private network (VPN) services that can be found in the App Store.

HOW TO TURN ICLOUD PRIVATE RELAY ON AND OFF?

Alongside the release of iOS 15, Apple also released a new service known as iCloud+. This service incorporates more functionality into Apple's premium iCloud plans (upgraded iCloud storage tiers begin at $0.99). One of these capabilities is called iCloud Private Relay, and it is intended to encrypt all of the communication that is leaving your device in order to prevent anyone from being able to read it or intercept it.

Web traffic that is routed through Private Relay is first sent to a server that is managed by Apple and then has its IP address removed. After the IP information has been removed, Apple sends the traffic to a second server that is maintained by a third-party company. This server assigns a temporary IP address to the traffic, and then sends the traffic to its destination. This is a process that prevents your IP address, location, and browsing activity from being used to create a profile about you.

Apple has stated that the decision to involve a third party in the relay system was a deliberate one and was made with the goal of preventing anyone, even Apple, from knowing either the identity of a user or the website that user is now navigating.

BONUS: MACBOOK SENIORS GUIDE

BONUS: iPhone 15 SENIORS GUIDE A COLORI

CONCLUSION

In conclusion, the developments in technology, particularly those that took place within the Apple ecosystem, have revolutionized the way in which we engage with the digital world and the devices in our possession. Apple continues to influence the landscape of the digital world in a variety of ways, including the seamless integration of Apple ID and iCloud, which offers improved ease, security, and personalization; the introduction of breakthrough technologies, such as Siri, which delivers virtual assistance to our fingertips; and the company's commitment to philanthropy.

In addition, the launch of HomeKit and automation via the Home app demonstrates the promise of smart home technologies, which in turn makes our living spaces more connected and efficient. It is imperative that we remain current with the most recent features and functionalities as we navigate these technological wonders. This will ensure that we are able to completely grasp the potential that these advancements have to offer.

Keep in mind that technology is just a tool; its true value rests in the ways in which it improves our lives and the connections we have with others. We are able to continue to take pleasure in a digital experience that is more savvy, more tailored, and more safe as long as we deliberately embrace these technological improvements and recognize their possibilities. Keep an open mind, investigate new functions, and be willing to adjust to the rapidly changing digital environment in order to fully take use of the amazing opportunities it presents.

Made in the USA
Las Vegas, NV
19 January 2024

84567984R00063